"Because of my involvement in baseball, and the rewards that come with it, some people are convinced I've got it made. But I have learned through painful experience that success is so much more than winning a championship or making a big sale. Dr. Charles Stanley is right: real success is a *process*. This powerful book will help you understand and achieve real, ongoing success—*Success God's Way!*"

Johnny L. Oates
Manager, Texas Rangers

"The spiritual guidance Dr. Charles Stanley provides in *Success God's Way* reveals that the path to true success is found only when we follow God's plan for our life. This book helps people succeed while staying committed to God."

Dick DeVos
President, Amway Corporation
New York Times Best-selling Author

"I totally agree with Dr. Stanley's *Success God's Way*. The principles are explained simply, all the techniques are in place, and it has all the answers for anybody who truly wants *Success God's Way*. Much respect."

Dexter R. Yager Sr.
Amway Crown Ambassador

"At last! Answers to questions every committed Christian asks about God's desires for His children. Dr. Stanley writes about success for the Christian clearly and concisely in his characteristic way of presenting biblical principles for practical, everyday life application."

Zig Ziglar
Author

"In an age where men and women seem *driven* to succeed in business, academics, and even spiritual pursuits, Charles Stanley defines success from God's perspective. In the clear, well researched style he is noted for, Dr. Stanley helps us take stock and reformulate our own goals and aspirations. Jeremiah 29 clearly says that God has a plan for our lives. *Success God's Way* helps us figure out how to get there from here. Practical yet inspiring, the life lessons in this book keep drawing us right into the father-heart of God."

Terry Meeuwsen
Co-host, *The 700 Club*

"This book gives such inspirational messages to hang in there when the road is tough, to persist when it seems we want to quit, and Dr. Stanley's ideas for pursuing God's goals for our lives encourage us to use our time constructively. Dr. Stanley shows how to adapt these principles for our lives in an exciting way. I think this book has a 'charm' about it that makes each page come alive with fresh ways to enhance our paths."

Barbara Johnson
Author, *He's Gonna Toot and I'm Gonna Scoot*

"In an age when our thinking is skewed, our zeal is waning, and our desire for excellence is deadened by apathetic self-centeredness, this book presents many biblical insights that challenge us to hear God's Word to Joshua to meditate on God's Word and be strong and courageous so we can have success."

Kay Arthur
Precept Ministries International

"Dr. Stanley has defined success in a timeless manner—knowing and doing the will of God. When a person knows Christ personally and consistently obeys the principles of Scripture, he is prepared for success God's way."

Franklin Graham
Author, *Rebel With a Cause*

"In a society that increasingly judges the success of individuals by the clothes they wear, the car they drive, the club they belong to, or the career they choose, the church desperately needs to reaffirm biblical standards. Once again, Dr. Stanley has brought clear focus to a timely issue. *Success God's Way* challenges readers to reexamine whether or not they are sacrificing genuine, lasting success on the altar of a worldly, temporary counterfeit and therefore settling for a lot less than what God wants to give them."

Anne Graham Lotz
International Bible Teacher and Award-Winning Author

SUCCESS GOD'S WAY

OTHER BOOKS BY CHARLES STANLEY

Enter His Gates
Eternal Security
The Gift of Forgiveness
The Glorious Journey
How to Handle Adversity
How to Keep Your Kids on Your Team
How to Listen to God

The In Touch Study Series

Advancing Through Adversity

Developing a Servant's Heart

Discovering Your Identity in Christ

Leaving a Godly Legacy

Living in His Sufficiency

Overcoming the Enemy

Protecting Your Family

Relying on the Holy Spirit

Talking with God

Understanding Financial Stewardship

Becoming Emotionally Whole

Developing Inner Strength

Experiencing Forgiveness

Listening to God

Ministering Through Spiritual Gifts

Preparing for Christ's Return

Pursuing a Deeper Faith

Sharing the Gift of Encouragement

Understanding Eternal Security

Winning on the Inside

In Touch with God
On Holy Ground
Our Unmet Needs
The Power of the Cross
The Reason for My Hope
The Source of My Strength
Winning the War Within
The Wonderful Spirit-Filled Life

SUCCESS GOD'S WAY

CHARLES STANLEY

OLIVER
NELSON
™

THOMAS NELSON PUBLISHERS®
Nashville

A Division of Thomas Nelson, Inc.
www.ThomasNelson.com

Published in Nashville, Tennessee, by Thomas Nelson, Inc.

Unless otherwise noted, Scripture quotations are from THE NEW KING JAMES VERSION. Copyright © 1979, 1980, 1982, Thomas Nelson, Inc., Publishers.

Scripture quotations noted NASB are from the NEW AMERICAN STANDARD BIBLE ®, © Copyright The Lockman Foundation 1960, 1962, 1963, 1968, 1971, 1972, 1973, 1975, 1977. Used by permission.

Library of Congress Cataloging-in-Publication Data

Stanley, Charles.
    Success God's way / Charles Stanley.
      p. cm.
    ISBN 0-8407-9142-9 (hc)
    ISBN 0-7852-6590-2 (pb)
    1. Success—Religious aspects—Christianity. I. Title.

BV4598.3 .S74 2000
248.4—dc21

                                    99-051387
                                    CIP

Printed in the United States of America.

05 06 RRD 14 13

CONTENTS

Introduction: God Desires Your Success   xi

1. How Do You Define *Success*?   1

2. God Is Committed to Your Success   13

3. The Key to Success: Setting Godly Goals   27

4. Stating Your God-Given Goals   47

5. A Personalized Pattern for Your Success   61

6. Pursuing God's Goals for Your Life   77

7. What About Money?   99

8. Roadblocks to Your Success   117

9. The Attitude Required for Success   141

10. Success Begins with an Idea   157

11. The Successful Use of Time   181

12. Overcoming the Negatives   197

13. Persisting Until You Succeed   217

Conclusion: Well-Ordered Steps   233

About the Author   237

Introduction

God Desires Your Success

Can success and a godly life truly be reconciled? Before I answer that question, consider the following people who seek to know more about success from a Christian perspective.

Jeff, age twenty-eight, sees his non-Christian friends moving up the corporate ladder at a rapid pace, while all of his Christian friends seem to be floundering in their careers. His non-Christian friends converse frequently about the latest success-oriented books they are reading to help them in their careers, while his Christian friends seem to care very little about personal success. He asks, "Is it right for a Christian to want to be a success in life?"

Karen, age thirty-five, sees her husband working forty-five hours a week, earning an honest wage for honest work while she stays at home—working as a full-time wife, mother, and homemaker. She knows that although they live a moral and upstanding life, are active in their church, and tithe regularly, they barely have enough money to make ends meet each month. In sharp contrast, Karen's friend Diane works full-time and has her children in day care, doesn't tithe or attend church, has a husband who is on a fast upward track, seems to make a number of moral compromises, and seemingly has lots of extra money for luxuries Karen can't dream of affording. Karen asks, "Can a person live a godly life and still be a success?"

Marge, age fifty, has worked forty years in the local factory and, in the opinion of most who know her, has had a hard life even though she has worked steadily and raised her three children to love God. As a single mother, she has routinely forgone the purchase of a new dress or an evening out with friends in order to help one of her children or grand-children with what she perceives to be a necessity. She asks, "Is God even interested in our being a success?"

Paul, age forty-five, thought he was secure in his upper-management position at the company where he had worked twenty years. And then he was downsized in a massive company reorganization scheme. He has been unable to find a comparable position in nearly a year of actively searching for work. Paul has watched his family's savings account shrink to half in that time. He asks, "Can we count on God to help us succeed?"

Many people ask these questions that Jeff, Karen, Marge, and Paul have asked. Generally speaking, Christians seem to ask these questions from one of two perspectives: either they have already concluded that God does not care about their success, although they still have a yearning to be success-ful, or they hope that God will allow them to be successful.

Most people seem to believe that success is limited to a certain group of people who bear distinct success qualities, or they believe that only a cer-tain segment of society has any hope of achieving success—and that seg-ment is not the segment to which they belong. Others firmly believe that success is something that can be attained only by those who are willing to lie, cheat, and steal from the common good, and therefore, success is not something a Christian should desire.

Very few Christians seem to believe in their heart of hearts that God truly cares about their success, desires their success, and is committed to helping them become successful.

In turn, those who are successful in the eyes of the world tend to look at many Christians and say with disdain, "I don't want to be like them." They, too, question or disbelieve God's desire for His people to be successful.

At the very outset of this book, I want to state that I firmly believe God desires for His people to be successful and that God not only desires this, but also is committed to helping His people become successful. In fact, most of the concepts that might be termed "principles for success" are ones that are based upon God's Word.

Success and a Godly Life

Is there a contradiction between being a success and living a godly life? Many people seem to think so. Those who promote success talk about making plans. The Bible, however, says, "Do not worry about tomorrow, for tomorrow will worry about its own things. Sufficient for the day is its own trouble" (Matt. 6:34).

Those who advocate success talk about exercising self-control and taking charge of one's destiny. The Bible teaches Spirit-control—being led by the Spirit into all things. Jesus taught, "When He, the Spirit of truth, has come, He will guide you into all truth" (John 16:13).

Those who preach success talk about having self-confidence, yet the Bible clearly teaches, "Have no confidence in the flesh" (Phil. 3:3).

Those who promote success speak in terms of getting to be number one or looking out for number one. They paint a picture of success as climbing a competitive ladder. They portray a dog-eat-dog world in which only those who are willing to use others can claw their way to the top. In sharp contrast, Jesus said, "Whoever slaps you on your right cheek, turn the other to him also. If anyone wants to sue you and take away your tunic, let him have your cloak also. And whoever compels you to go one mile, go with him two" (Matt. 5:39–41). The apostle Paul taught that Christians are to walk "with all lowliness and gentleness, with longsuffering, bearing with one another in love, endeavoring to keep the unity of the Spirit in the bond of peace" (Eph. 4:2–3). We read in James 4:10, "Humble yourselves in the sight of the Lord, and He will lift you up."

At the beginning of this chapter, I asked, Can success and a godly life truly be reconciled? Absolutely! The key lies in our definition of *success* and our deeper understanding of how God desires for us to be successful. We must begin with a *Bible-based* definition of *success* if we truly want to be a success—God's way.

1

How Do You Define *Success*?

How do you define *success*? If you are going to achieve success, you first must know what it is you are aiming to achieve!

A football coach might define *success* as winning a national championship.

A salesman might define *success* as being number one in the company.

A college student might define *success* as earning a degree.

A homemaker might define *success* as having a lovely home.

A businessman might define *success* as earning a million dollars a year.

A parent might define *success* as raising godly children.

Definitions tend to come and go, depending on whom you ask and when you ask.

For Scott, success was defined as living the good life. By the time he was thirty, he was in business for himself, working between seventy and eighty hours a week. He was married with two children, drove the luxury car of his choice (and his wife, the car of her choice), and had a house in the suburbs. He went to church at least once a month, which he thought was sufficient to expose his children to the Bible stories in Sunday school. He also went deep-sea fishing, his only hobby or recreational pursuit, at least once a month.

Scott had as his foremost goal to retire in a house at the beach by the time he was fifty, primarily so he could fish as often as he wanted.

Generally speaking, many people define *success* as "setting a goal and accomplishing it." That definition, however, is limited. A person might set an evil goal or a good goal. The nature of the goal is a key factor in success, especially if we are dealing with *God's* view of success.

Our human approach to success tends to be: here's my goal. God's approach is: here's the person I want you to be, here's what I want you to do, and here's how to be that type of person and how to do that task. It is in *being* a godly person and then *obeying* God in His directives that we find success as Christians. Our life as Christians is not to be wrapped up in what we possess, earn, or own. Life for Christians is wrapped up in who we *are* in Christ Jesus.

On the surface, it may be easy to criticize Scott for having a shallow goal, one that really didn't include the whole of his life. Scott, however, would have said otherwise. He had been raised in church and believed in Jesus Christ. He had received God's forgiveness at the age of twelve while attending a church youth camp. He considered himself to be a born-again Christian. That's the main reason he went to church once a month—so that his spiritual obligation to his children might be fulfilled. He had a desire—yes, perhaps even a goal—that his children be saved.

But Scott had never faced the fact that God desired more for him and from him than the acceptance of Jesus Christ as Savior. He desired for Scott and his entire family to follow Jesus Christ as *Lord*—to base all of their goals and desires on what the Lord had as goals and desires for their lives.

A Continuing Desire to Pursue God's Desires

First, and foremost, we must recognize that as believers, we are the sons and daughters of the living God. Success from God's viewpoint does not begin and end with what we *do* in our lives. It begins and ends with who we *are* as His children. Here is the definition of *success* on which this book is based:

> Success is the continuing achievement of becoming the person God wants you to be and accomplishing the goals God has helped you set.

From the perspective of this definition, ungodly persons cannot be genuinely successful. Ungodly people might amass a certain degree of material wealth, achieve a certain degree of fame, gain a certain number of degrees or awards, attain a certain level of social privilege or status, or garner a certain degree of political or social power, but the ungodly are not truly successful in their lives because they are not becoming the people God has called them to be. They are achieving their goals, not God's goals.

The ungodly are defining their lives according to their lusts, desires, and purposes rather than seeking to line up their lives with God's desires, plans, and purposes. People cannot be successful from God's viewpoint and leave God out of their lives. The same is true for those who call themselves Christians but who rarely, if ever, consider the plans and purposes God may have for them.

The world tends to sum up success in terms of fame and fortune. God sums up success in terms of relationship, character, and obedience. He desires for us to succeed first and foremost in our relationship with Him, then in our relationships with others, and then in our vocations and ministries.

Does this mean that godly people cannot experience fame, fortune, power, social status, accomplishments, notoriety, material gain, or rewards? No. It means that in the arena of success, the *processes* and the *purposes* of God-focused people are very different from those of the self-focused. The self-focused person begins with self-gratification, self-definition, and self-made goals. The God-focused person begins with God's plan and purposes.

The self-focused person is concerned primarily with success that can be measured in terms of dollars, awards, and outward displays of wealth, prominence, and status. The God-focused person is concerned primarily with success that begins *within* and is defined in terms of eternal purpose, spiritual benefit, godly character, abiding satisfaction and fulfillment, and obedience to God's commandments and daily directives. The godly person may experience as side benefits wealth, prominence, and status, but these are not primary goals and objectives. They are by-products and blessings bestowed by God.

Scott fell into the trap of becoming a self-focused person. By the time he was thirty-three, his company was flourishing. He and his family had moved to an even bigger house in a nicer neighborhood, and they had joined a country club. Scott began to move in bigger circles finan-cially—ones in which certain behaviors seemed expected. He began to smoke cigars for the first time in his life and to become a connoisseur of wines. He had a bar built into his new home for entertaining, and he took a bartending course to learn to concoct every drink his guests might order.

Scott and his wife, Bryn, took their vacations where their new friends vacationed, mostly at spas and exotic resorts. Scott rationalized all that he was doing under the umbrella that it was "good for business"—the busi-ness that was going to lead to his early retirement. He enjoyed the fact that he was making a name for himself, not only in his chosen career field but also in his community.

Scott and Bryn went to church occasionally—if nothing else was planned—and they sent their children to vacation Bible school and church camp.

Things seemed to go along fine for a couple of years, but then things began to crumble, just a little at first. When their daughter turned four-teen, signs of rebellion emerged. Scott had a scare medically that the doc-tor diagnosed as a stress reaction. He took prescription medications to control his anxiety. As his business grew to even greater size, Scott spent seven days a week at work. Bryn, feeling neglected, spent time with those who were "available" to sit by her new pool, including a single man with whom she later had an affair.

Scott and Bryn eventually separated to sort things out in their marriage, and as problems with their children, Bryn's affair, and Scott's drinking escalated, their separation led to a divorce. By the time he was thirty-eight, Scott was fighting a difficult divorce-settlement battle over his business and possessions, becoming increasingly estranged from his children, and struggling to control his blood pressure and anxiety attacks.

Was Scott successful? Those who looked at the outside of his life might have said so. He was the CEO of a thriving business, wore expensive suits, drove a late-model luxury car, and took clients to lunch in all the right restaurants. But inwardly? Scott felt like anything *but* a success. And from God's point of view? Well, Scott was giving very little thought to God's point of view.

The real rewards associated with God's success are the intangibles that all people want. The self-focused person may think he desires fame and fortune. But in the end, every person has as his deepest desire inner peace, joy, contentment, health and wholeness (spirit, mind, and body), feelings of spiritual security, the hope of eternal life, family love, and a living relationship with God. Scott was woefully short of the things that really mattered.

On more than one occasion, I have heard a very wealthy or famous person, who is considered to be a success by others, say, "I'd trade it all for a little tranquillity and a secure hope that I know what is going to happen to me after I die."

On more than one occasion, I have heard the sick and dying say to me, "I'd trade all the success I've achieved for an hour of pure love, an hour without pain, or an hour of knowing that I have done what God created me to do."

Those who limit their pursuit only to fame and fortune wind up frustrated and disappointed, with a gaping void in their lives that they cannot fill. Those who choose first to pursue the life for which God designed them and to which God calls them experience the real richness of life and the joy and hope associated with an everlasting life.

Scott eventually hit bottom. A major conglomerate bought out his business, and with the money he retained for himself, he bought a small house at the beach and took stock of his life. He realized all that he had lost in the process of seeking gain, and he recognized that the most important thing he had lost was feeling close to God.

Scott recommitted his life to following Jesus Christ as Lord. He began to attend church regularly, to pray, to read his Bible, and the more he did so, the more he longed for his wife, his children, and a life that he realized he had always desired but had never really had. He asked the Lord daily, "What do You want me to do?" Scott didn't leave his house in the morning until he felt he had an answer from the Lord to that question.

At first, the Lord seemed to lead Scott into volunteer work through his church. He became involved in Habitat for Humanity projects, hammering and sawing and building homes for people in need. The fresh air and hard physical labor helped clear Scott's mind as he continued to grapple with what the Lord had for him and his family.

Scott made face-to-face contact with Bryn and his children after not seeing them for six months. He discovered that Bryn had ended her affair and had been going through a similar soul-searching time.

Did things automatically fall back into place for Scott? No. It took two years of steady Christian counseling before Scott and Bryn were reunited in marriage. It took two more years of Christian counseling before Scott could truly say that his relationship with his children was healed and restored. In those years, the family experienced difficult times periodically. But one thing had changed—Scott's attitude toward what was truly important in life. Every morning, Scott continued to ask the Lord in prayer, "What do You want me to do today?"

Scott is now in his mid-forties. He is very active in the men's ministry of his church, and four times a year, he leads deep-sea fishing retreats for fathers and sons. Many people who go on the retreats are unsaved, and a good percentage of those men and their sons accept the Lord while at sea with Scott.

Bryn leads a women's Bible study in her church and works part-time at a crisis pregnancy center. Both children are attending Christian college, and their once-rebellious daughter is preparing for her first full-time job with a teen ministry that sponsors missions trips.

Scott is in business again, on a smaller but adequate scale, using the profits from his business to fund projects at church, including underwriting the fishing retreats he conducts.

Is Scott a success? He feels he is, I believe he is, and I believe *God* sees Scott as successful. The foremost reason for Scott's success: he still asks the Lord every morning, "What do You want me to do today?"

There is no more important question you can ask related to your success.

Our Ongoing Pursuit of Success

Success is an *ongoing pursuit*. It is establishing and accomplishing and forever seeking to establish and accomplish the God-given goals the Lord sets for our lives. It is refusing to become discouraged, disheartened, or dissuaded from God's goals. It is the result of the *continuing* desire to be the person God calls us to be and to achieve the goals that God helps us to set.

No person ever truly achieves success. Success is not a quantity that can be measured or a concept that can be fully defined. It is a concept embedded in a *process*. Our understanding of success continues to grow as we mature in Christ. It continually lies ahead of us and continually develops within us.

Can we ever reach the horizon? Can we walk enough miles or sail enough miles to get to the edge of the world? No. The more we walk the earth or sail the sea, the more the horizon extends before us. And so it is with success. It is always just beyond our grasp, compelling us, calling us, urging us onward. That's the way the Holy Spirit works in our lives. He allows us to experience great joy and satisfaction in the present moment of our lives, and at the same time, He calls us to greater conformity to Christ Jesus, greater desires for ministry, and greater tasks in the establishment of God's purposes on the earth.

Am I saying that God is opposed to wealth? Absolutely not. God says very clearly in His Word that He is the Source of all wealth.

Is God opposed to your becoming somebody who is perhaps famous or who has an outstanding reputation in your field? No, He is not opposed to that.

What is God opposed to? God is opposed to your trying to live your life while ignoring Him. God is opposed to your trying to be something that you can never be apart from Him.

When a person attempts to achieve something apart from God, he spends energy and time in pursuit of what cannot produce lasting happiness and peace and joy. He may live in a palatial home, drive the finest automobile, and have a large bank account and a full portfolio of stocks and bonds, but unless he has eternal security born of a relationship with God, he is a failure. He is not a success in the eyes of God.

Many of us are going to be surprised when we get to heaven and see who *God* says is a success and who is a failure. Their names are never going to be in anybody's book or newspaper or on anybody's television program here on earth, but mothers who raised godly children are going to hear God say, "You are a success. You are a faithful and good servant. Great is your reward."

People who have worked at jobs forty years, paid their bills, lived honest lives of integrity, tithed to the Lord, and participated in church outreach programs but never have won an award, earned a community honor, received group applause, or been labeled a success by anybody for anything are going to hear God say, "You are My successful servant and friend. Great is your reward."

On the other hand, people who have struggled greatly to create careers for themselves and to become people of notoriety and fame but have had no time for the things of God, no time for church, no time to develop a relationship with the Lord Jesus Christ are going to hear the Lord say, "I don't know you. Nothing you have done or earned or made of yourself has value to Me."

Friend, I wouldn't swap places with anybody in the world who has money, notoriety, or power but doesn't have God. What he has won't matter in the least five hundred years from now. What will matter is whether he can call Jesus Christ his Savior and Lord.

As believers, we never arrive at a place where we can say, "Aha! I'm here. I'm a success. Now let me sit down and enjoy life and rest on my laurels."

Rather, we always have a hunger in our hearts to be more like Christ, to draw closer to the heart of God, and to know more about the truth God presents in His Word. We have a thirst to taste more and more of the goodness of God. We have a desire to serve Him with greater consistency, efficiency, and focus. We have a desire to bear more and more fruit that has eternal reward associated with it.

Does this mean that we live in a constant state of unrest and frustration when it comes to success? No! And that is the great mystery of God's plan for success. As much as the ideals of God's success lie ahead of us and urge us forward in our Christian walk, the satisfaction that the Lord imparts to our hearts grows. We live in a greater and greater state of contentment, regardless of our circumstances or the obstacles that confront us. We grow in God's peace and in our ability to abide in the Lord with the assurance that nothing can separate us from His presence and His love.

The self-focused person strives continually for greater and greater success, more and more wealth, more and more fame, more and more power.

The God-focused and spiritually mature person is freed from striving. He lives in a steady state of confidence—confidence in God's power and presence, confidence born of relationship with God—while at the same time living in the hope of greater and greater things that God will unfold and reveal and bestow.

I have never met a financially wealthy person who wasn't a little fearful at the prospect of losing his wealth, or who didn't desire to amass even more wealth "just in case."

I have never met a famous person who wasn't a little concerned that his latest movie, record, project, or accomplishment wasn't his "last" great effort. Most famous people know that the public is fickle and that fame must continually be fueled by new successes.

I have never met a corporate leader who wasn't looking for the next deal, the next alliance, the next takeover to ensure that his corporation remained the leader and that he remained at the top of his corporate ladder. Corporate leaders live with a take-over-or-be-taken-over tension.

I have never met a political leader who wasn't concerned with reelection or, in the case of someone who desires to retire or who has retired from politics, with the legacy of accomplishment in history. Political leaders know that power is fleeting.

The external trappings of success don't last or endure over time. Certainly the marks of external success might last months, years, decades, or a century or more. But they do not extend into eternity. Nothing that man does on his own power and for his own purposes extends into eternity. Only the things that bear the seeds of God's presence last into eternity.

Which brings us back to our original definition of *success*:

Success is the continuing achievement of becoming the person God wants you to be and accomplishing the goals God has helped you set.

Genuine success—from God's point of view—is rooted in what *God* calls us to be. It is rooted in what *God* sets as the goals for our lives. It is rooted in our relationship with God, who enables us to become the people He created us to be and to do the works He has authorized us to do.

When we seek success from God's point of view, God is 100 percent committed to our success. We can count on it!

2

GOD IS COMMITTED TO YOUR SUCCESS

When I first met Kyle, he was the picture of dejection. He gave me a limp handshake and collapsed wearily in the chair opposite me. I thought perhaps he was ill. But then he said, "Pastor Stanley, I just don't get it. I'm trying to live a good Christian life out there in the business world, but I just don't think the honest guy can get ahead. Every time I turn around, I see a good person getting stabbed in the back, and lately I've been the one getting stabbed. It seems to me that those who care the least about God are the ones who are getting the promotions, raises, and all of the perks. I don't see any evidence at all that God cares one bit about whether I or any other Christian succeeds."

If that is the way you feel today, let me assure you, as I assured Kyle, God is committed to your success. God *wants* you to succeed and stands ready to help you succeed beyond your greatest dreams.

How do I know this? I believe there are three main forms of evidence:

First, God has given us all of the principles for genuine success in His Word. He has made the knowledge of how to be successful available to every person.

Second, God has built into each person a desire for success.

And third, God has given each person talents and gifts that, when developed and employed, yield the benefits of success.

Let's take a closer look at each one.

The Bible Is God's Success Manual

Over the years, I've probably read two or three dozen books on the subject of success. Some of them have included God in their discussion, and a few have put God at the center of a successful life. But I discovered that, without exception, every genuine principle of success in these books can be found in the Bible.

The principles of success are not foreign to a godly life; rather, they are embedded in a godly life. The world may think it has discovered this idea or that idea about success, but in truth, God is the author of all success, and God's Word has presented success principles for human living for thousands of years.

The word best translated "success" appears in the Bible only seven times—twice in Joshua, and once each in Genesis, Nehemiah, Job, Ecclesiastes, and Daniel. No word directly translated "success" appears in the New Testament. We might be tempted to conclude from the lack of Bible references directly linked to success that God is disinterested in the success of His people. Such a conclusion, however, would be erroneous.

Rather than use the word for success, the Bible uses the word for "prosper." To prosper in all you do is to succeed in all you do. To be prosperous is to be successful. Anytime we read about the Lord prospering His people, we can be assured that the Lord is helping His people to succeed in all ways. For example, John wrote, "Beloved, I pray that you may prosper in all things and be in health, just as your soul prospers" (3 John 2).

Whole-Person Prosperity

The success or the prosperity that God has for you is always a whole-person prosperity. Note again in 3 John 2 that the prayer of John was that the people would prosper in all things—their material, social, natural, financial, outer lives—just as they would prosper in their personal health and their spiritual lives. The prosperity he desired for them covered their entire lives. It was prosperity that might be described as "wholeness in action."

Take inventory of your life today. Ask yourself:

- Where am I in my spiritual walk?
- Where am I in my finances?
- Where am I in my vocation?
- Where am I in my service to the Lord?
- Where am I in my health?
- Where am I in my relationship with other people, including my family, my friends, and those with whom I am involved at church and at work?

God desires for you a success that will touch every aspect of your life. He desires for you to become whole and, in wholeness, to prosper in all areas of your experience.

Notice also that John prayed that the Lord's followers would prosper outwardly as their souls prospered. How many of us truly want to prosper to the degree that our souls are prospering? Frankly, most people I encounter hope that the Lord will prosper them in their finances and material lives far more than their souls are prospering. If they were to prosper financially only to the degree they were prospering spiritually, they'd be living in poverty.

The Lord links outer and inner prosperity, and the clear implication is that the Lord is going to prosper us financially, in our work, in our relationships, and in our material lives only to the degree that we are prospering spiritually or in proportion to our spiritual prosperity.

Consider the person who desires to prosper financially but fails to obey God when it comes to giving his tithes and offerings to the work of the Lord. Is the Lord going to be committed to helping a person who is disobedient in the use of finances to prosper financially?

When the Lord sees slothfulness and sloppiness and laziness in our lives, He cannot be committed to prospering those character qualities.

When the Lord sees a misuse of resources or a failure to be good stewards of our income, including a failure to give what we are commanded to give, the Lord cannot be committed to prospering us financially.

Our success always has conditions on it, and the conditions are primarily spiritual.

Wholeness is independent of circumstances. The Bible also teaches about prosperity that our wholeness—our inner and outer prosperity—depends not on outer circumstances but on our inner-faith relationship with the Lord.

Perhaps no person faced more difficult circumstances for his entire life than Daniel. Daniel was taken into captivity by the Babylonians as a young man. He was transported to Babylon and forced to live in an alien culture the rest of his life. He served under three heathen kings—Nebuchadnezzar, Cyrus, and Darius.

Not only did Daniel face death when the magicians of the king failed to interpret the king's dream—something Daniel later did after the Lord revealed the dream and its meaning to him—but he faced a den of lions for being faithful in his prayer life. Few of us have ever faced, or ever will face, ongoing circumstances as negative or as harsh as those faced by Daniel. And yet we read in Daniel 6:28, "So this Daniel prospered in the reign of Darius and in the reign of Cyrus the Persian." Daniel lived well and lived successfully in the midst of his circumstances. And that is precisely what we are called to do.

One of the principles at the foundation of Bible prosperity is faith. Every success book I've read states, in one form or another, that a person has to believe he can be successful. The principle of faith is a constant for success. The real question for Christians is this: Faith in what or in whom? It is only when we identify the object of our faith that we truly know the foundation for our success.

If you put your faith in yourself and your abilities, intellect, and dreams, then your foundation is only as strong as you are. And no matter how strong you may be, you are neither omnipotent nor omniscient.

If you put your faith in God, then your foundation is as strong as He is, which is all-powerful and all-knowing.

God's Call to Success

Not only do we find God's desires for our success expressed in the Bible, but we find numerous examples of people whom God called to be successful.

God called Joshua to be successful. Not only was Joshua to be successful personally in his leadership role, but all the Israelites under his leadership were called to success. We read in the first chapter of the book of Joshua:

After the death of Moses the servant of the LORD, it came to pass that the LORD spoke to Joshua the son of Nun, Moses' assistant, saying: "Moses My servant is dead. Now therefore, arise, go over this Jordan, you and all this people, to the land which I am giving to them—the children of Israel. Every place that the sole of your foot will tread upon I have given you, as I said to Moses. From the wilderness and this Lebanon as far as the great river, the River Euphrates, all the land of the Hittites, and to the Great Sea toward the going down of the sun, shall be your territory. No man shall be able to stand before you all the days of your life; as I was with Moses, so I will be with you. I will not leave you nor forsake you. Be strong and of good courage, for to this people you shall divide as an inheritance the land which I swore to their fathers to give them."

[The Lord spoke to Joshua,] "Only be strong and very courageous, that you may observe to do according to all the law which Moses My servant commanded you; do not turn from it to the right hand or to the left, that you may prosper wherever you go. This Book of the Law shall not depart from your mouth, but you shall meditate in it day and night, that you may observe to do according to all that is written in it. For then you will make your way prosperous, and then you will have good success. Have I not commanded you? Be strong and of good courage; do not be afraid, nor be dismayed, for the LORD your God is with you wherever you go." (Josh 1:1–9)

What a tremendous statement of God's desire for Joshua and the Israelites to be a success! What a tremendous statement of God's commitment to help Joshua and the Israelites achieve success!

At the opening of the book of Joshua, God told Joshua that He was giving him the awesome responsibility of leading a nation of more than two million people across the Jordan River into the land that God promised them. Twice in the opening chapter, God said, "This land will be yours— it will be your territory, your inheritance." Twice, God said to Joshua personally, "No man will be able to take over your position of leadership. You will be successful in the role to which I have called you."

The real question is not whether God has promised success to you if you are faithful in following His principles related to success. The real question is, Are you willing to accept and believe that God desires your success?

Nehemiah believed in God's commitment to success. Nehemiah was a man in the Bible who believed and claimed God's success for himself. Nehemiah was a servant of the king, and when he heard news that the walls and gates of Jerusalem were in ruins, he fasted and prayed about the situation.

The king noticed the sorrow in Nehemiah's countenance, and he asked him why he was sad. Nehemiah explained the situation in his homeland, and the king offered to give Nehemiah everything he needed to go to

Jerusalem and make repairs to the city, including an escort to ensure his safe passage to Jerusalem and back.

Once Nehemiah arrived on the scene, he faced opposition from those who did not want him to succeed in the task before him. We should never be surprised when we face opposition. Any person who is doing the will of God is going to face opposition from the devil and those whom the devil can influence. Read how Nehemiah responded to the opposition:

> I told them of the hand of my God which had been good upon me, and also of the king's words that he had spoken to me. So they said, "Let us rise up and build." Then they set their hands to this good work. But when Sanballat the Horonite, Tobiah the Ammonite official, and Geshem the Arab heard of it, they laughed at us and despised us, and said, "What is this thing that you are doing? Will you rebel against the king?" So I answered them, and said to them, "The God of heaven Himself will prosper us; therefore we His servants will arise and build, but you have no heritage or right or memorial in Jerusalem." (Neh. 2:18–20)

The God of heaven Himself will prosper us. Is that your attitude today toward your success? Are you truly believing that God is on your side and that He is committed to your success?

Success Is a Process

Too often we look at the people in the Bible and conclude, "But I'm not like that." The fact is, we *are* like the people in the Bible, and they were like us in their responses to life, their struggles, their successes and failures, and their personalities and desires. The human heart has not changed. Technology and places may change, but the human heart has not changed through the ages. What you feel, the people of the Bible felt. What you think, the people of the Bible thought.

Did Jesus' apostles have days that seemed mundane and drab? Of course!

Were all of the days of Moses glorious? No!

Was every moment of every day a high point for any one hero or heroine of the Bible? Certainly not.

For most of our lives, and their lives, the days are marked by sheer obedience, persistence, endurance, and struggle. Most days are not ones of either glowing success or devastating failure.

The point is this: achieving success does not mean that you are going to live on the top of the mountain with a big grin on your face and a blue ribbon attached to your lapel every moment of every day of your life. High points may come. They may be frequent at times and virtually nonexistent at other times.

Success is not based on how you feel or on the uplifting moments when you receive rewards, recognition, or overwhelmingly positive responses from others. Success is to be found in the way you live day in and day out. It is to be found as you *pursue* what God calls you to be and to do.

Success is not the end of a process. Success is *how we undertake the process* called life. God's Word is our guidebook for the journey.

A Built-In Desire for Success

Not only has the Lord given you His Word to challenge, call, and compel you to success, but He has built into you a deep desire for success.

Every child comes into this world goal oriented. Take a look at a baby in a crib who begins to cry and is given a pacifier. He may suck on that pacifier for a little while, but the next thing you know, he is playing with it, and before long, he has pulled the pacifier out of his mouth and it has rolled just beyond his reach. The baby might squirm a little or raise his arm in hopes of reaching that pacifier, but when his efforts fail, what does that baby do? He begins screaming and crying again! He is goal oriented even in the crib, even for a pacifier. That child will do everything in his power to get his needs satisfied.

Every normal, healthy baby comes into this world with a desire to achieve and succeed in life—to do and have the things that will bring a sense of satisfaction and fulfillment and contentment. He has a desire to communicate and express himself, a desire to relate to others, and a desire for mobility—to scoot, to crawl, to walk.

God has given you an inbred desire for success so that you will *act.* He has given you the desire so that you will motivate yourself to discover your gifts and talents and use them. You have a built-in drive to get your needs met in a way that brings pleasure.

Some people seem to have been inbred with the idea that they should always be taken care of or that handouts from others are the way to live. To live with a reliance upon others is not God's design. Rather, it is a *choice* that people make, consciously or unconsciously.

Some people choose defeat, choose to fail, choose to be lazy, choose not to care, and choose to blame others continually for their own lack of success. To a certain degree, these people have made a choice to live by manipulating others, guilt-tripping others, or using others for their purposes. They don't have any less desire to live a good life—they have chosen ungodly means for attaining that good life. (Manipulating others, imposing guilt on others, and using others for selfish purposes are *not* in line with God's plan. They are methods of the enemy, not methods that God calls righteous.)

The drive that God builds into you is neutral. It can be directed into lust of the flesh, lust of the eyes, and the pride of life. Or it can be directed into a pursuit of the things of God and the success that God has planned for you. But the drive toward success, satisfaction, and fulfillment is present in you—it is a gift of God to you that He expects you to use in right ways.

God Has Equipped You for Success

In addition to the promises of God's Word and the desire for success God has built into you, God has equipped you with one or more natural talents and abilities as well as one or more spiritual gifts (which are also called motivational or ministry gifts). These gifts have been embedded in your unique personality for one reason—so that you might use these gifts to the best of your ability and produce quality work that has a potential for both earthly and eternal reward.

Let's take a closer look at the process involved in the use of your gifts. The first step is the discovery of your unique gifts. If you do not know what God has gifted you to do, study your life and abilities. You may benefit from taking certain aptitude or spiritual gifts tests. Discover what God has built into you.

The second step is the development of your gifts. Gifts do not emerge full-blown and at peak perfection. Your talents, abilities, and spiritual gifts must be developed through practice, application, and exercise. You become better at your talents, whether they involve playing the piano or functioning in the spiritual gift of exhortation, the more you *employ* your gifts.

The third step is yielding your gifts to the Holy Spirit. At the time you trust in Jesus Christ as your personal Savior, God gives you the presence of His Holy Spirit in your life. One of the functions of the Holy Spirit in you is to empower what you do in the name of Jesus and to cause what you do in the Lord's name and for His glory to produce eternal fruit.

The Holy Spirit in You Enables Your Success

The Holy Spirit functions in many ways to help you become successful as you practice and use your gifts. One way is to heighten your ability to discern right from wrong, good from evil, and to make choices among good alternatives. As you face decisions regarding when and where and how to employ your talents and spiritual gifts, ask the Holy Spirit to help you in the decision-making process. Ask Him to help you discern the way in which you are to go.

Another way in which the Holy Spirit helps you is to empower you to use your gifts to their maximum effectiveness. All work takes effort and energy. The Holy Spirit helps you by renewing your strength, sharpening your senses, and helping you to do the greatest amount of work in the least amount of time in the most efficient manner. What you think you can do well on your own strength and ability, you can do much better when you actively rely on the Holy Spirit's help.

Yet a third way the Holy Spirit helps you is to give you His comfort and reassurance that all things are working together for your good from God's perspective (Rom. 8:28). Too many people waste precious time and energy worrying about whether they did enough, did well enough, or did the right thing in the use of their talents and spiritual gifts. They second-guess virtually everything they have done or are about to do. The Holy Spirit assures you that when you use a talent or spiritual gift with a right motive of love toward God and toward others, He will take what you use and mold it and edit it and transform it into something that is effective, beneficial, and applicable.

A fourth way the Holy Spirit helps you is to nudge you in the direction you should go and toward the people you should touch with your talents or spiritual gifts. Some say the Holy Spirit *convicts* them about the direction they should take, the words they should say, the deeds they should do. Others say the Holy Spirit *moves* them to do certain things, and still others say the Holy Spirit *compels* them to act in certain ways. Whatever term you use to describe the guiding power of the Holy Spirit in your life, the fact is, the Holy Spirit seeks to guide you daily into the ways in which you should walk and the activities in which you should engage. Listen closely to how He leads you.

Now if I said to you that I was sending a person to help you make wise decisions for the greatest amount of success, to empower your work so that you will function at maximum capacity, to ensure that all of your efforts are effective and beneficial, and to motivate you continually, you would no doubt accept the help of that person eagerly and enthusiastically. Well, the Holy Spirit has been sent to do all of that in you and through you. When you ask the Holy Spirit to help you in the use of your talents and spiritual gifts, He *makes* you effective and successful.

It doesn't matter if you are a schoolteacher, a homemaker, a plumber, a carpenter, an attorney, a doctor, or a business executive—God wants you to succeed at the tasks ahead of you. He has built into you the abilities and talents and spiritual gifts necessary for you to do your job exceedingly well, consistently well, and effectively. And He has sent the Holy Spirit to ensure that your use of your talents and gifts will be successful.

Never Discount What God Has Given You

Too many Christians do not move into the full success that God has for them because they discount the gifts of God.

Never underestimate or discount yourself or your abilities. If you have the Lord Jesus Christ as your Savior and the power of the Holy Spirit resident in you, you can do *all* things that the Lord leads you to do. To underestimate yourself or sell yourself short is to underestimate God in you and to sell His abilities short.

Never belittle yourself. In criticizing or saying negative things about yourself, you are also saying critical and negative things about Christ in you.

Never count yourself out. As long as you are alive and the Lord is resident in you, you are very much "in the game."

Never use your race, your color, your lack of education, or your background as an excuse. God knows all about your race and color and culture—He caused you to be born with that race and color and into that culture. What you don't know, God knows. What you don't have, God has.

Never use your age as an excuse for not pursuing success. God doesn't have a retirement age for you. You may change your vocation at age sixty-five or seventy or seventy-five, but you are still to live and minister to others and set goals as the Lord directs you to set them and then do what the Lord leads you to do. You are to bear fruit in your old age (Ps. 92:14).

Never use circumstances as an excuse for why you aren't pursuing God's goals for your life. Are you aware that most of the people who have accomplished anything truly worthy in life have come from difficult circumstances? The struggle and strain and stretching and refusing to give up in the face of difficult circumstances create the very qualities that make people successful. God knows all about your circumstances, and He will enable you to overcome them.

I recently heard about a young blind woman who had enrolled in a college that was not particularly easy for any person to navigate, much less a person who was blind. A reporter for the college newspaper asked her if she found the campus a major challenge. She responded, "Every day of my life is a challenge. Every day I have to move about in spaces that are new to me. This college is just one more unknown space I must explore. I have trusted God all my life to help me move about safely, so I'll just continue to trust Him to help me move about safely here."

This young woman certainly didn't let the circumstance of blindness keep her from her goal. Her courage had been built up over the years—one day at a time—to handle the challenge ahead of her.

The Power of Prayer Is Related to Your Success

Not only has the Lord given you the Holy Spirit to enable your success, but He has given you the powerful privilege of prayer. You have the privilege of bowing before God every single morning and saying, "Lord, I need You to guide me today. I need Your help. I need Your strength. Show me how to get along with this person. Show me how to rally the troops. Show me how to be motivated toward my family and toward my job in the balance that You desire."

The Lord delights in your prayers requesting His help. He delights in your prayers of faith and uses them to move aside the obstacles that stand before you. He uses your prayers to thwart the evil intentions of others against you, to destroy the works of those who seek to persecute you, and to demolish the devil's efforts to destroy you and steal from you. God has given you a very powerful tool in prayer—it is a tool that activates the forces of heaven on your behalf and builds a wall between you and the forces of hell.

Intended for Use!

God put His principles and promises for success in the Bible for one purpose—so that you might believe them, learn them, and use them.

God has built a desire for success into your life so that you will act.

God has built gifts and talents into your life, given you the Holy Spirit, and given you the tool of prayer so that you might use your gifts, follow the leading of the Spirit, and pray with faith that God's will for your success and the success of others will be accomplished.

God does not only want you to know how to be successful in theory; He has given you all you need to be successful in reality.

3

THE KEY TO SUCCESS: SETTING GODLY GOALS

~❧

If you knew with absolutely no doubt that you could not fail in accomplishing your choice of three goals, which three goals would you set for your life?

In your present spiritual condition could you honestly ask God to help you achieve those goals?

Do you really want God's very best for your life, or are you willing to settle only for what you can do on your own?

Do you really want the *best* that God could provide for your life?

These questions lie at the heart of a Christian's pursuit of success. They are the questions that lead each of us to ask, What goals does *God* desire for me to set and to achieve and, in the process, to be a success in His eyes?

A Continual Pressing Toward God's Goals

One of the most goal-oriented people in the Bible is the apostle Paul. In writing to the Philippians, Paul spoke plainly about the number-one goal he had set for his life:

What things were gain to me, these I have counted loss for Christ. Yet indeed I also count all things loss for the excellence of the knowledge of Christ Jesus my Lord, for whom I have suffered the loss of all things, and count them as rubbish, that I may gain Christ and be found in Him, not having my own righteousness, which is from the law, but that which is through faith in Christ, the righteousness which is from God by faith; that I may know Him and the power of His resurrection, and the fellowship of His sufferings, being conformed to His death, if, by any means, I may attain to the resurrection from the dead. Not that I have already attained, or am already perfected; but I press on, that I may lay hold of that for which Christ Jesus has also laid hold of me. Brethren, I do not count myself to have apprehended; but one thing I do, forgetting those things which are behind and reaching forward to those things which are ahead, I press toward the goal for the prize of the upward call of God in Christ Jesus. (Phil. 3:7–14)

Paul was not a man who wasted time or energy. He was extremely focused in his life. He had an overwhelming sense of purpose and direction.

Prior to his conversion, Paul was focused on the destruction of Christian believers. His goals were of his own creation and were not of God. After his conversion, Paul was focused on a new set of goals—goals that were in keeping with *God's* desire for his life. He summed up those goals for the Philippians:

- Knowing Jesus Christ as intimately as possible and experiencing His righteousness in his own life

- Knowing the power of Christ's resurrection and being conformed to Christ in every way, including His sufferings and death

We know that both goals were also manifested in a third goal of the apostle Paul:

- Reaching as many people as possible with the name of Jesus and the message of His crucifixion and resurrection, and doing so as quickly as possible, as efficiently as possible, and as irresistibly as possible

Early in Paul's ministry we find this statement: "As they ministered to the Lord and fasted, the Holy Spirit said, 'Now separate to Me Barnabas and Saul [Paul] for the work to which I have called them'" (Acts 13:2). That "work" was the preaching of the Word of God in the synagogues of the Jews in Salamis on the island of Cyprus. That was the beginning of Paul's missionary work, a work that occupied the remainder of his life and kept him traveling throughout the region, preaching, teaching, and establishing churches wherever he went.

Paul made no claim that he had achieved his goals, but stated that he was continuing to press toward the goal of the prize of the "upward call of God in Christ Jesus." To press on means to diligently follow after. Paul was zealous in following Christ. Just as a runner stretches every nerve and muscle in his body, and longs to be in peak performance as he goes to the track each day, so Paul desired for everything within him to be stretched and honed to perfection in following Christ.

Paul was continually pressing to experience more of Christ and more of Christ and more of Christ. Paul's foremost goals were knowing Christ in His fullness and experiencing everything he could of Christ.

What are your goals today? What are you pressing toward?

Setting Godly Goals

A goal is an aim, a purpose, or a sense of direction toward which you move all of your energies, desires, and efforts. Goals give rise to specific objectives, purposes, or aims. Goals are the targets toward which you point your life.

A goal involves an organized, planned stretching of your life. A goal is a statement of intention that you seek to grow, develop, mature, or change in a positive, specific, and achievable way.

Goals for Christians are based upon an understanding that we do not live for ourselves. Rather, we live as unto the Lord. Are you fully aware, and fully convinced, that you do not belong to yourself alone? As a believer in Christ Jesus, you have been bought with a price, the precious blood of Jesus Christ (1 Cor. 6:19–20). You are now the possession of Jesus Christ. You belong to Him. You have a life that He expects you to invest in the things of God, a life that is expected to bring glory to God.

Establishing a Priority Goal

The priority goal for the apostle Paul was to know the Lord Jesus Christ in a personal, intimate way, and to know Him to the degree that he would be conformed completely to the likeness of Christ Jesus. The Bible tells us that God has this same priority goal for each one of us. In Romans 8:29–30 we read,

> For whom He foreknew, He also predestined to be conformed to the image of His Son, that He might be the firstborn among many brethren. Moreover whom He predestined, these He also called; whom He called, these He also justified; and whom He justified, these He also glorified.

Every other goal must be placed under this priority goal—to know Christ and to be conformed to His likeness. If you have set for yourself a goal that is not in line with this priority goal, God will not help you accomplish it because He didn't encourage you to set it. If a goal cannot be placed under this supreme goal of knowing Christ and being conformed to His character, that goal is *contrary* to God's purposes for your life, and God will oppose you in your attempts to achieve it.

Do I personally have a priority goal? Absolutely. My goal is to know Christ as intimately and fully as possible. My secondary goal, and one that sets the pattern for my life and determines the details of my daily schedule, is this: to get the gospel of Jesus Christ to as many people as possible, as clearly as possible, as quickly as possible, as irresistibly as possible, by the power of the Holy Spirit and to the glory of God. Period. That's *why* I live.

That goal motivates me to get up in the morning and work hard all day and often well into the evening and night. That goal drives my other priorities. That goal compels me to stay as healthy and as vibrant and as strong as I can be. That goal motivates me to search continually for new ways of expressing the gospel and new avenues to pursue for the distribution of the gospel message.

I'd much rather preach the gospel forty more years than twenty more years. If I die tomorrow or in the next five minutes, I know my heart is right with God and I will be with the Lord. But my *desire* is to live many more years in pursuit of the goal that I believe God has given to me. I am content in my life today, yet I desire to do so much more to extend the gospel around the world.

Is your first goal a desire to know Christ and to be conformed to His likeness? If your first goal is a desire to know Christ, your other goals are likely to be ones that God will honor. If your goals have nothing whatsoever to do with Christ Jesus, I encourage you to reevaluate your thinking and your goal setting. Take another look at what it truly means to you to be a success. Do you want to be a success according to God's definition or according to your definition?

Does having this priority goal of conformity to Christ limit you in your goal setting? Absolutely not. If anything, it *expands* your thinking when it comes to setting godly goals!

All of these goals fit with God's priority goal for every Christian:

- To walk in the Spirit daily
- To experience the same kind of awesome Holy Spirit power that Jesus Christ experienced

- To serve God in the fullness of the Holy Spirit's guidance and power

- To maximize my full potential

- To use all of my talents and abilities in the way God created them to be used

- To fulfill God's purpose for my life

- To experience and enjoy life to its fullest

- To have a feeling of deep and abiding satisfaction that I have fulfilled God's goals for my life

- To know the joy that comes in knowing Christ

The Benefits of Having Goals

What do goals do for you? They help you set priorities. Some things become vitally important, while others cease to have any importance.

Goals help you focus your efforts. They keep you from getting off into stray topics, relationships, and activities that serve as distractions and sometimes deterrents.

Goals help you set your schedule, not only over long periods of time, but daily. A person with goals doesn't want to waste time.

Goals help you balance your life. Staying healthy and feeling good—which involve proper nutrition, adequate sleep, times of relaxation and recreation, and daily exercise—become important because they are linked to the ability to accomplish goals. Spiritual life becomes supremely significant because the only goals truly worth having are linked to an eternal purpose and eternal reward. Involvement with others in the church and in the business world enables a person to do more than he can do by himself, whether participating in direct ministry outreach or providing the funds necessary to fuel a ministry outreach.

The Qualities of a Person with Goals

What are the qualities of a person who has goals for his life?

A person with goals has direction for his life. He is going somewhere. He is not frivolously meandering through life.

A person with goals has an excitement about life. He has exuberance and an inner motivation that say, "I'm glad to get up in the morning and eager to start on this day's plan." Daily goals nearly always seem to take on more meaning because they are linked to longer-range goals and the priority goal. Goals are very often linked directly to a will to live. A person with goals feels needed and believes that life is worth living.

A person with goals has remarkable energy. There is an energy level in the life of a person with goals that is missing from a person who has settled for a settled-down life. A person with goals often works ten or twelve hours a day because he doesn't want to quit in the pursuit of a goal. He rarely checks the time because he is intent upon the tasks at hand or the relationship that is being forged.

A person with goals is often very creative. Part of what our Creator builds into each of us is a creative drive—a drive to initiate new projects, businesses, or ministries; to try something new; or to produce something unique. Every person is given a unique, one-of-a-kind set of talents, dreams, desires, propensities, aptitudes, and spiritual gifts. The blend is intended for a creative purpose so that the person might express his unique qualities in a unique way. When a person pursues God-given goals, he feels creative sources flowing from deep within. His mind hums with ideas about how to do things, and he tries new approaches and methods to address old problems.

A person with goals pursues excellence. A person who is actively seeking to accomplish a God-given goal is likely to want to accomplish that goal to the very best of his ability. He is invested in his goals, and he desires to see them accomplished with an excellence of method, an excellence of spirit, and excellence as the hallmark of the product, service, or result.

A person with goals has a great sense of appreciation for others who have goals and who are pursuing them to the best of their ability. He enjoys being around successful people. He desires for others to become successful. He enjoys sharing what he knows with others who desire to learn from his experience and talent.

A person with goals tends to be physically healthier than a person without goals. The person with goals wants to feel good. He works at staying healthy because he values his life and wants to live to see his goals accomplished. He desires to do what is necessary so he can stay strong and function at peak mental ability. He disciplines himself to have the sustaining energy to get the job done that he believes God has led him and is enabling him to do.

A person with goals tends to be emotionally healthier than a person without goals. The person with goals has a sense of contentment, enjoyment, satisfaction, and happiness. He has very little inclination to get bogged down in feuds, arguments, disputes, or disagreements. He lives with less bitterness and does not fuel feelings of anger, frustration, and disappointment. He is more concerned with what lies ahead than with what has been hurtful in the past.

The Qualities of a Person Without Goals

What are likely to be the qualities of a person who has no goals? Think about such a person for a moment. He is likely to exhibit the following characteristics:

A person without goals generally has no excitement in his life. He has no enthusiasm for getting up in the morning. He has no ambition to make the most of every day. Nothing energizes him.

A person without goals is drifting through life without a sense of direction. The person with no goals tends to drift along through life, never accomplishing much and never really seeking to do anything. Such a person tends to live from day to day, hand to mouth, taking life as it comes and doing little to change negative circumstances. He may attach himself to anything enticing that comes his way, including things that are negative and even evil just for the sake of having something to think about or something to do. He accepts mediocrity as a way of life.

A person without goals is often very critical of others, especially those who are successful or who are working hard to achieve particular goals. The person without goals basically doesn't like himself very much. He doesn't believe he is worthy of achieving anything or doing anything remarkable. To make himself feel better, he tends to criticize others, hoping to bring them down to his level. He is especially critical of those who are pursuing goals, often ridiculing them as "trying to be big shots" or "being money hungry" or "chasing after a dream." He enjoys watching others fail or struggle with obstacles because he feels more justified in his own laziness and unwillingness to take risks in the pursuit of goals.

A person without goals tends to settle for living in a rut. He claims to like consistency, but he actually is afraid of change and challenge. He is willing to settle for the routine. The person who opts to live in a rut is virtually closed in his spirit to any challenge of the Lord to grow, mature, or develop. Such a person rarely hears God's call to reach new people with the gospel or to extend himself to participate in a new ministry outreach.

A person without goals winds up living a disappointing life. When he looks back over his life, he feels dejected that he has so little to show for his time on this earth. He has a sense that he has wasted his life—wasted resources, wasted time, wasted energy, wasted gifts.

I truly believe that to live a life without the pursuit of goals is to sin against God. It is to shut off all challenges of God to extend oneself to others. It is to be a very poor steward of the precious gift of life that God has given to each one of us. And it is to live in disobedience to God's call to grow in Christ Jesus, to mature in Christ, and to be conformed to Christ. It is to deny that God's initial purpose and plan for a person's life were valid, and it is to turn away completely from the potential that God has placed inside each person.

Which Do You Choose to Be?

Look at the overall picture of someone who has goals and someone who doesn't:

PERSON WITH NO GOALS	PERSON WITH GOALS
• Adrift	• Sense of direction
• No excitement in living	• Excitement about life
• Accepts mediocrity	• Pursues excellence
• Critical of others who are successful	• Appreciates others who are successful
• Disappointed with existence	• Strong sense of purpose, value, worth
• Settles for living in a rut	• Seeks a creative, active life
• Poor steward of God's gifts of time, resources, energy	• Seeks a balanced life marked by emotional and physical health

Which type of person do you believe God desires for you to be? Which type of person are you?

Why People Fail to Set Goals

If goals are of such positive benefit to us and so much in keeping with the quality of character that the Lord desires for us to develop, why don't all Christians have goals? Why aren't all Christians pressing toward the call of Christ in their lives?

I believe there are several reasons.

Some Engage in Self-Disqualification

One of the foremost reasons people do not set or pursue goals is that they don't believe success or goal setting applies to them.

For example, a homemaker might say, "Oh, I'm just a homemaker. I live day to day to meet the needs of my family." A homemaker can and should have goals. Nothing about being a homemaker replaces or negates having godly goals. Consider these goals that are in keeping with a priority goal of knowing Christ and are also possible goals of a homemaker:

- To raise children who will grow to love the Lord Jesus Christ, accept Jesus as their Savior, and have a good knowledge and understanding of the Bible and how to apply its principles to their daily lives

- To create a home that is truly a haven of safety, comfort, and encouragement for every member of the family

- To create a home environment filled with joy and the peace of the Lord

- To create a beautiful, clean, and well-appointed home that is a testament to God's creative, gracious, well-ordered creation

- To create a family schedule that allows for good stewardship of time for each family member—including times for work, sleep, play, study, conversation, and quiet

What wonderful goals these are for a homemaker!

Some may say, "I'm ninety years old now. What goals could I possibly have?"

A person can set many goals for himself regardless of age. An older person should perhaps be the first to set such goals:

- Keep my body as fit as possible, eating nutritious, healthful foods, exercising daily, and getting sufficient sleep

- Keep my mind as alert as possible, reading and studying new things, and using my mind to solve problems and to make wise, well-researched decisions

- Keep my spirit strong through daily reading of God's Word and prayer not only for myself but as an intercessor for others

- Keep my relationships with my family members and friends alive through frequent, positive, interdependent contact

- Keep my ministry gifts active, using my spiritual gifts in every way possible at my church and in my community

- Keep my natural talents alive through continued practice and use of the skills I acquired earlier in my life.

There are no age limitations on such goals!

Some Lack Knowledge

Some people fail to set goals because they don't know how to set goals. They erroneously believe that goals are dreams. The two are vastly different.

A dream is a desire, a hope, a wish. It is often rooted in an unfulfilled fantasy or something imagined in childhood. This is not to say that dreams are unimportant or unworthy of being pursued. To the contrary, our dreams are very often the seeds that give rise to goals. Every person needs to have dreams.

A goal, however, is a dream that is set into the context of time. A goal makes a dream concrete. It puts specific parameters around a dream.

Let me give you a few examples:

- DREAM: To be a missionary.
  GOAL: Research missionary organizations, and undertake whatever is necessary to be on the mission field within three years.

- DREAM: To start a business that brings glory to God.
  GOAL: To be the owner of a Christian bookstore within five years.

- DREAM: To become involved in Christian media.
  GOAL: To get a job working for a Christian television or radio station within six months.

As a young boy, I had a dream that I wanted my life to count for something. I wanted to do something important and worthwhile in my life, but I didn't know exactly what that might be.

As I became a teenager and prepared to go to college, I began to question, What really matters to me? I pondered what truly seemed important and worthwhile to me. The more I gave thought to it, the more I realized that I wanted to preach the gospel. Telling others about Jesus and teaching what the Bible has to say about the Christian life became the most important things I could imagine doing.

People sometimes ask me, "Dr. Stanley, when and where did the Lord call you to preach?" My answer is that the Lord called me to preach by stripping away every other occupation as being unimportant, uninteresting, and unnecessary—not to others, but to *me*.

What do you dream of doing?

What goals are connected to that dream?

Some Are Too Lazy

Some people know how to set goals, but they are too lazy to do so. They are mentally slothful. They don't want to have to think about the importance, value, or worthiness of their own lives. They don't want to have to get up out of their easy chairs and do what the Lord might challenge them to do.

I asked a man what goals God was leading him to pursue, and he responded, "My only goal now is to retire in ease. I've already done most of my life's work. I'm tired. My goal is to take it easy for a while."

The man was in his late fifties! I couldn't imagine that he truly thought he had accomplished most of his life's work. He may have needed a vacation or a few months away from his corporate job in order to regroup his strength and his zest for living. From my perspective, however, he needed to have a long talk with the Lord to set some new goals for his life that would get him out of his ease and into productivity for the extension of God's work on this earth.

Some Lack Faith

Many people have goals—often unspoken ones—about what they would like to do with their lives. Some never take the first step, however, to turn those goals into plans and then work their plans. Why? They don't believe they can accomplish what they want to do. They would rather do nothing than attempt something they are not sure they can achieve.

I'd rather try something I know I cannot accomplish without lots of help—and fail—than spend my life doing only those things I know I can succeed at using my own resources.

We are called to take risks and to have faith. If we could do everything on our own, without God and without the help of others, we would have little need of God. God has built into us an ability and a desire to set goals that are just beyond our reach and beyond our ability to attain them in our own strength. He has done this so that we will need to trust in Him and to rely upon Him to do for us what we cannot do for ourselves. He calls each of us to live by faith and, as the apostle Paul wrote to the Corinthians, to "walk by faith, not by sight" (2 Cor. 5:7).

Some Fear Failure

Others have goals, but they don't act on them because they are afraid. They may be afraid of failure. They may be afraid of rejection by other people. They may be afraid that they will disappoint others or themselves.

We each must learn to distinguish between *being a failure* and *failing at something*. I may be defeated in a particular game, but that doesn't mean I'm a failure. I may still reach the goal of a league championship, even with several game losses. The point is to keep trying. A person never fully fails unless he gives up. As long as a person continues to pursue a goal, there is the possibility of success in achieving it.

All of us fear failure. It's at that very point that we are called to turn to God, to use our faith, and to move ahead with courage.

We must also recognize that our failures can ultimately be for our benefit. Many people learn more from their failures than they do from their successes. They learn what doesn't work, what not to do, and what not to pursue. God often allows defeat in the life of a believer in order to guide that believer into the path in which he should walk and into the path in which he will succeed.

A cancer researcher once said, "I have just completed a third experiment that didn't turn out the way I had hoped." A reporter asked him, "Are you discouraged?" He responded with a laugh, "Oh, my, no! I am encouraged. I know three more things that are *not* effective in fighting this particular type of tumor. I'm three steps closer to what *will* work."

Some Are Shortsighted About the Future

Some people are able to plan for today or tomorrow, but they can't seem to envision goals farther in the future. Unless they are dealing with something such as buying a house or a car, they can't imagine making plans or entering into agreements that extend beyond their next paycheck.

The Bible certainly tells us that we never know what a day may bring and that we are to live day by day, but I believe the greater truths in the Bible are these:

- We must trust God to meet our daily needs and to guide us through the circumstances we will encounter each day.

- We must not carry vengeance or unforgiveness beyond the day. We must not go to bed angry or allow bitterness to take root in our hearts. We must forgive others quickly.

- We must live each day to the fullest, taking advantage of every opportunity afforded us to extend the gospel and to fulfill the godly goals we are pursuing.

41

Some Believe That Goal Setting Is Unscriptural

Some in the body of Christ contend that Christians should not set goals. They cite several passages of Scripture to support their belief. I want to take a look at each of these passages.

The Argument for Contentment. The first passage often used in the teaching that goal setting is not scriptural is Hebrews 13:5: "Let your conduct be without covetousness; be content with such things as you have. For He Himself has said, 'I will never leave you nor forsake you.'"

This verse has nothing to do with whether a person should set goals or have godly ambitions. The admonition to "be content with such things as you have" is in direct relationship to the statement to "let your conduct be without covetousness." We are never to covet what someone else has, including the success of another person. One of the Ten Commandments states, "Thou shalt not covet." Our lives must never be driven by a desire to acquire things or by a love of money.

If a person's idea of success is to get all the money he can so that he can be secure, he has missed the mark. Our security can never be based upon money because financial wealth comes and goes, fortunes rise and fall, phenomenal estates and vast financial empires can crumble overnight. Our security lies solely in Christ Jesus, who says to us, "I will be with you always. I will never desert you. I will never forsake you."

A related verse used in teaching against goal setting is Philippians 4:11: "Not that I speak in regard to need, for I have learned in whatever state I am, to be content."

What is contentment? *Contentment is the realization that God has provided all that we need for our present happiness.*

Happiness and goal setting are not synonymous. Happiness and success are not synonymous. Contentment is the realization that God is the Source of all that we need for our present happiness.

Philippians 4:11 does not advocate that we settle down and remain satisfied with our current level of achievement and our current level of ministry and our current level of spiritual growth. Far from it! This verse is from the same Paul who just a few verses before this one wrote, "I press toward the goal!"

One of the great mysteries of the Christian life is that we can be very content and at the same time press toward more goals that the Lord has laid upon our hearts to achieve and accomplish. We can experience both contentment and a desire to press onward and upward because our contentment is based upon Christ's presence in us. Our relationship with Christ allows us to be content *in* all situations and at the same time desire to change our situation.

Many people talk about the good old days. I have yet to meet a person who truly wants to go back and live in those days, however. They don't want to read by candlelight or wash their clothes on a washboard. They don't want to go back to using manual typewriters or doing mathematical calculations without the aid of an adding machine, calculator, or computer.

Does that mean that people who lived in the good old days were discontented? No, not really. Those who knew Christ experienced great peace, joy, and contentment in their souls. But thank God, they also had a desire to invent the electric lightbulb, the washing machine, word processors, and handheld calculators!

Contentment has to do with your attitude—to be content is to know that you can rest in the Lord and trust Him to help you with every situation and every goal. Contentment is living free of worry and anxiety. It is living free of anger and bitterness and resentment of other people. It is living in peace with God, your heavenly Father. It is knowing that you are forgiven and that you will live forever in heaven.

Contentment is knowing that no matter what any person may do to you—torture you, persecute you, ridicule you, or even kill you—he cannot separate you from God's love and forgiveness.

Ask yourself today,

- Am I satisfied with what I know about God? Or is there more that I still desire to know?

- Am I satisfied with the depth and intimacy of my relationship with Christ? Or is there more that I still desire to experience in my relationship with the Lord?

- Am I satisfied with what I know about God's Word? Or is there more that I still desire to learn and apply to my life?

- Am I satisfied that I am fulfilling to the best of my ability all that God desires for me spiritually? Or is there still more that I believe the Lord desires for me to do?

- Am I satisfied that I am using my spiritual gifts to the best of my ability? Or is there more that I can be doing to express Christ Jesus to the world in which I live and in the church to which I belong?

As Christians, we are, and should be, content in knowing that Jesus is our Savior and that we are eternally secure in Him. But we must never be content with the level or degree of our spiritual maturity and the degree to which we have become conformed to Christ. There is always room for growth—and it is in the area of what can be and the area of more growth that we are to set goals as God directs us.

God places in every genuinely born-again Christian an insatiable hunger and thirst to know Him better. We can be genuinely contented and delighted and satisfied with the Lord and, at the same time, have a deep desire to grow, understand more, and become more intimate with the Lord. That's the way God made us. To deny our desire to grow and mature and deepen our relationship with God is to put ourselves in a situation in which we are likely to feel the very opposite of contentment.

The Argument About Living Each Day as It Comes. Matthew 6:31–34 is another passage that is often used to counteract a need for goal setting:

[Jesus taught,] "Therefore do not worry, saying, 'What shall we eat?' or 'What shall we drink?' or 'What shall we wear?' For after all these things the Gentiles seek. For your heavenly Father knows that you need all these things. But seek first the kingdom of God and His righteousness, and all these things shall be added to you. Therefore do not worry about tomorrow, for tomorrow will worry about its own things. Sufficient for the day is its own trouble."

Jesus is not teaching about planning or not planning in this passage. This passage of the Bible has to do with worry—feeling anxious about whether the Father will meet our day-to-day needs for food, shelter, and clothing. Jesus' answer is a resounding, "Yes! The Father cares. He will meet your needs!"

Jesus also says that we are to seek *first* the kingdom of God and His righteousness. I believe that one of the foremost ways in which we seek the kingdom of God is to ask the Lord to help us set goals that are directly related to His kingdom and the pursuit of righteousness. The first goals we should set are related to our spiritual growth, the use of our spiritual gifts, our spiritual outreach or ministries, and our daily spiritual disciplines.

As the apostle Paul wrote to the Colossians, you are challenged to "seek those things which are above, where Christ is, sitting at the right hand of God. Set your mind on things above, not on things on the earth" (Col. 3:1–2).

Paul wrote to Timothy, "Pursue righteousness, godliness, faith, love, patience, gentleness. Fight the good fight of faith, lay hold on eternal life, to which you were also called and have confessed" (1 Tim. 6:11–12).

Your top goals should relate to inner character and things that yield eternal reward.

Four Questions to Ask About Goals

As you set goals for yourself, I believe there are four key questions you should ask:

First, ask God, "Why is this important to You, Lord?" If you understand the answer to the *why* question about your goal, you'll be in a prime position to seek answers to all of the other questions: *how, when, where,* and *with whom.* Listen closely for the answers God gives you as to why He desires for you to do certain things or to display certain character traits. You'll gain insight into the broader plans and purposes of God.

Second, ask about every goal you set, "Does this fit into Your plan for my life?" Some tasks and goals are very important to the Lord, but He does not ask *you* to undertake them. They may be tasks not in keeping with your natural or spiritual gifts. Or they may be tasks and goals that are good but not God's *best* for you. Ask the Lord what is right for *you* to pursue.

Third, ask yourself, Is this goal totally in line with God's Word? God will not lead you to pursue a goal that is contrary to His Word. He will not violate the principles of His Word in *how* to pursue a goal. Neither will He lead you to seek a goal that will in any way detract from your conformity to the character of Christ. Always check your goals against God's Word. They should line up perfectly.

Fourth, ask about each goal, How might the accomplishment of this goal bring blessing to others? God gives us goals so He might do two things simultaneously—He desires to perform a refining work in your life, and perform a work that will benefit others and be for their eternal good.

With this perspective on setting goals, the time comes when you need to write down your goals. That's the first step in turning what you believe to be true about goals into a statement of God's goals for your life.

4

STATING YOUR GOD-GIVEN GOALS

The Lord places great value on our writing down the things that He speaks to our hearts or that He challenges us to do.

The prophet Jeremiah was told on several occasions to write down the words of the Lord. In Jeremiah 30:2, we read, "Write in a book for yourself all the words that I have spoken to you." In Jeremiah 36:2, the Lord was even more direct: "Take a scroll of a book and write on it all the words that I have spoken to you."

The Lord told the prophet Habakkuk:

> Write the vision
> And make it plain on tablets,
> That he may run who reads it. (Hab. 2:2)

It is not enough for you to daydream in your thought life about the things you'd like to have as goals. A goal must ultimately be a *statement of intention.*

Goals Must Be Set in the Context of Time

In addition to writing down goals, you should set them in the context of time. A true goal has an end point within a particular time frame. Therefore, goals tend to be of three types: immediate, short-range, and long-range goals.

Immediate Goals

These tend to be daily or weekly goals or perhaps even goals that will take a month.

I have an immediate goal each week of preparing a sermon that will meet the needs of my congregation. I seek to prepare a sermon that is easy to understand, easy to follow, and hard to forget. I want to prepare a message that others can apply to their lives; I want my message to be one that makes note taking easy.

Regardless of the time frame set for any goal, the goal needs to be broken down into tasks that can be done on a daily basis.

"To become more physically fit" might be among your long-range personal goals. That goal, however, needs to be turned into things that you can do daily, such as "exercise today" and "eat right today."

Every evening, I make a list of things that I believe I should do or that I want to do the following day. Do I get everything done on my daily list? Oh, I wish I did! I rarely mark off everything on my list. But I refuse to become discouraged. The next evening, I scratch off the things I did and add the things I didn't do to the next day's list. A daily list keeps me focused on the things that are truly important for me to accomplish. The list helps me set my schedule and remain true to my priorities, and it reminds me that I want to develop certain habits, cultivate certain relationships, and accomplish certain things in the near future. (I'll share more about the value of making a daily list in Chapter 11.)

Short-Range Goals

These goals usually take a month or three months or even a year.

Not too long ago, I set a short-range goal of taking a photography trip to a wilderness area. I especially enjoy taking photos of nature. These photos are a creative way for me to express my praise to God and to express to others the appreciation and joy I feel about God's creation. Planning a trip several weeks in advance was a short-range goal.

Long-Range Goals

Long-range goals usually extend beyond a year. They include life-long goals.

I believe it's better for most people to keep their long-range goals to themselves, but that in no way should become an excuse for not making long-range goals. We need to have things we'd like to do in the years that lie ahead.

I rarely tell people about my long-range goals. I'd rather accomplish them and then look back and say, "I've been working on this for several years." In keeping with that approach, I am happy to tell you that I recently accomplished one of my long-term goals.

For years, I enjoyed taking photographs, but I had no real goals about photography. Finally I enrolled in a seminar in New England to learn specific techniques and principles. I had made a decision that I wanted to excel in photography. I started setting goals, and one was that I wanted to publish some of my photographs in the books I was writing. I have now reached that goal.

For us as Christians, our long-range goals are likely to include the following: win as many souls to Christ as possible, earn the maximum heavenly reward possible for our faithfulness in pursuing Christ's call on our lives, and fulfill our purpose on this earth as a "good and faithful servant." Eternal goals are the ultimate long-range goals!

Goals for Every Category of Life

Not only should we have goals that fall into different time frames, but we also should have goals for different areas of our lives. I personally set goals in these six areas:

1. Spiritual
2. Personal
3. Family
4. Vocational
5. Social
6. Financial

Let me give you several examples of goals that might fall into each of these areas:

1. Spiritual. Spend more time reading God's Word; spend more time in prayer (immediate). Share the gospel with at least five people in the next month; start a Bible study in my home in two months (short-range). Renew my musical skills and play in the church orchestra by this time next year; take a one-year course on the gospel of John; teach in vacation Bible school next summer (long-range).

2. Personal. Join a gym and start a regular exercise program (immediate). Go on a trip with a group of Christians to Israel next fall (short-range). Finish a graduate degree (long-range).

3. Family. Spend time with my son on the golf course this weekend (immediate). Coach my daughter's Little League team this coming season (short-range). Put all of my children through college (long-range).

4. Vocational. Make five sales calls today (immediate). Be the number-one salesman this month (short-range). Be promoted to district manager (long-range).

5. Social. Invite a friend to dinner this week (immediate). Get involved in an outreach to older members of my church (short-range). Take each of my godchildren on a special vacation trip before they turn eighteen (long-range).

6. *Financial.* Start tithing (immediate). Save to be able to purchase a car within twelve months (short-range). Get completely out of credit-card debt within two years (long-range).

Goals can easily be put into a grid, such as the one here. I encourage you to use this grid in identifying your goals:

	IMMEDIATE	SHORT-RANGE	LONG-RANGE
Spiritual			
Personal			
Family			
Vocational			
Social			
Financial			

Ask the Lord to Direct Your Goal Setting

The key for a Christian in goal setting is this: ask God to guide you as you set goals. Don't put down things that you think would be fun to do, good to do, or even "spiritually righteous" to do. Ask God what He desires for you to do—specifically, immediately, in the near future, and in the long run.

Begin any goal-setting session in prayer. Don't do all the talking. Listen carefully to what God may speak to your heart. Never underestimate what God wants to do for you, in you, or through you. Listen to what *He* brings to your mind and heart.

And then continue to mull over and pray about what the Lord seems to be leading you to establish as goals. Open your Bible and study particularly the passages that relate to the goals God seems to be nudging you to set. Spend some time contemplating the gifts and talents, and especially the spiritual gifts, that God has given you. Ask the Lord to give you a picture of *how* you are to use your talents and spiritual gifts and in which areas He desires for you to employ your gifts immediately.

Be especially concerned with what you set as a long-range goal. A long-range goal will tend to direct and guide a series of immediate and short-range goals that are like steps toward accomplishing your long-range goal.

Back in the very early 1970s, I went to Stone Mountain near Atlanta in our travel trailer, and I spent an entire week asking God one question, "What do You want me to do with my life?" I fasted, prayed, and wrote down things that God seemed to speak to my heart. I was very serious about wanting to know what *God* wanted me to do.

There were times when I'd write down something but think, *Well, now, that's an egotistical thing to write down.* But as I prepared to erase what I had written, God would speak to my heart, *No, keep that in writing. That's of Me.* There were other things that I thought I should write down or that I would have liked to write down, but the more I thought about them and prayed about them, the less I was interested in writing them down. I can't even recall now what some of those things were. They became totally unimportant to me. When I got back home, I typed out each goal I had written in a complete sentence that began, "In my life, I am going to . . ."

Through the years I've reviewed that list of goals more times than I can count. I have added a few things, but for the most part, that list remains intact. And I don't mind telling you, with very few exceptions, I'm still working on each one of those goal statements! In a few cases, the things I had set as goals seemed to be accomplished, but then as I prayed about the particular goals, the Lord seemed to set even higher standards or higher goals in a related field. The goal didn't really change, and it wasn't met fully. Rather, the goal expanded and developed and, in some cases, diversified a little.

A good long-range goal is likely to be one that you never reach fully and that expands over time the more you pursue it. It is likely to be a goal that is worthy of your pursuit all through your life. Rather than be accomplished, it may take on different expressions and characteristics over time. Nevertheless, it is a goal that abides.

"But what," you may ask, "if I write down a goal and it's not of God?" Before long, you will have an empty feeling about that goal. The more you pray about it, the less interested you likely will be. Scratch it off your list. If it truly is a goal from God, He will bring it to your mind and heart repeatedly. If it is not of God, you will think of it rarely and perhaps never again.

If you write down a goal and you then feel uneasy about it—restless in your spirit, troubled in your mind, questioning without answers, a nagging feeling in the pit of your stomach—go to God again and say, "Lord, have I heard You correctly on this matter, or is this just my own idea?" Listen closely to what the Lord says to you.

You are going to make mistakes in goal setting. Nobody is going to get the list right the first time. As you live out your lifetime goals—turning them into immediate and short-range goals, and living them out on a daily basis—you begin to discern which are godly goals and which are goals that fuel your lusts and fleshly desires.

Other Principles Related to Goal Setting

After you have your statement of general goals as the result of asking God for His guidance, you should do several other things in setting goals:

State Precisely What You Intend to Accomplish

Don't deal in fuzzy generalities. Be specific. Don't just say, "I want to join a Bible study." Name the study, give a time frame for joining it, and note how long you intend to participate in it.

When Jesus encountered Bartimaeus at the outskirts of Jericho, He asked Bartimaeus one simple question: "What do you want Me to do for you?" (Mark 10:51). Jesus could see that Bartimaeus was blind. He was dressed like a blind man. He stood before Jesus with eyes that could not see. Yet Jesus asked him the question.

The reason for the question was not so that Jesus might know the need. The reason was so that Bartimaeus might face his need and his healing squarely. Great responsibilities came with being healed—Bartimaeus would be expected to work, to participate fully in the life of his family, his synagogue, his city. He no longer would live off alms or the generosity of his family and neighbors.

By writing down our goals in specific and concrete terms, we have a clearer understanding about what we truly want. One woman said to me after filling in a grid related to goal setting, "I've already erased five things. I thought I wanted those things until I really thought through how much time and energy they would take and how little spiritual reward they might produce. I thought I knew what I wanted until I wrote down what I thought!" That often is the case.

You also need to state your goals in terms that can ultimately be measured. If you write down a goal and there is no way of knowing when you have achieved it, you have not written a clear goal statement. For example, "Be a better person" is not a good goal statement. "Be a better person by this time next year" is not a good goal statement. What is your definition of a *better person*? What does that mean in terms of what you will do, especially in relationship to others?

"Read my Bible more" is not a good goal statement. "Read my Bible every day" is a better statement because it can be measured, but it still isn't concrete enough. "Read my Bible through from cover to cover this year, reading at least half an hour each day" is a good goal statement. A specific amount of energy and time is associated with that goal statement. It will be easy for that person to tell if he is achieving his goal and if he has achieved it fully by year's end.

"Get more education" is not a good goal statement. "Go to college" is more specific, but still not specific enough. "Finish college in four years" is a clear goal statement that can be measured.

"Save money" is not a good goal statement. "Save enough money to put a down payment on a house within eighteen months" is a goal statement that is clear, concise, and measurable.

Keep Your Goals Private

As much as I encourage you to write down your goals, I also encourage you to keep your goal statements private. One closet in my home is *my* closet. Nobody goes in there but me. And on the wall of that closet is my list of goal statements. I know exactly where that list is and what each goal says. My list is a matter between God and me.

If you publicize your goals to others, you set yourself up for criticism—not only related to your choice of goals, but also related to your failure to reach some of your goals in a timely manner. Your goals should be a matter of trust in and obedience to God.

There may be some things you would like to do, but you cannot see how they are related to your eternal purpose or your priority goal of knowing Christ and being conformed to His character. For example, you may say, "I want to see the Swiss Alps and travel to Australia in my lifetime." You may even feel good about setting a time frame for those trips. "But what," you may find yourself asking, "does this have to do with the Lord?"

Ask the Lord what it may have to do with Him. The Lord may want you to go on a short-term missions trip to one of these places, or He may call you to go to these locations to pray and intercede for the people there. Perhaps He has in mind another purpose for your visiting these places. If you have had the desire to visit a particular place and it is an abiding desire over time, ask the Lord why He has placed that desire in your heart. Listen closely for opportunities that He may reveal to you related to your desire.

Very often when I have set goals, I have discovered that the godly purpose I saw in the accomplishment of the goal and God's true purpose did not turn out to be the same at all. His purposes were much more important than my purposes.

One young man I know had a strong desire to visit Russia. He saved his money and went there as a tourist. He felt called to intercede for the people as he traveled. On several occasions he had an opportunity to share the gospel. He thought his desire and his purpose in going to Russia had been fulfilled.

But do you know what happened to him when he came home? He couldn't get the Russian people off his mind. The more he prayed for them, the more he thought about them, and the more he thought about them, the more he felt led to pray for them. An opportunity opened for him to go on a short-term mission trip to teach in a Bible school in Russia. He went. And he thought that surely he had fulfilled God's purpose in his going to Russia. But God had more. The young man eventually went back to Russia as a missionary and has served there now for several years.

What happens if you don't reach a goal in the time frame you set for it? Don't be discouraged! More than likely you will reach some goals before the due dates you have established, but you won't reach others for some time after the dates you've set. What matters most is not that you accomplish a goal on a certain date, but that you work continually toward your goal. Ultimately the time frame is God's.

Set Goals You Can't Reach on Your Own Strength and Ability

I encourage you to set some goals so high, you can't possibly reach them without God's help. Set goals that stretch you, challenge you, and cause you to expand and develop all of your gifts—both natural and spiritual—

in new ways. A true God-given goal is going to be a goal that you *and* God can accomplish, but that you cannot accomplish solely on your own.

Make a Commitment to Your Goals

Don't write down a goal that you don't truly intend to work at achieving or that you don't intend to pursue with your whole heart. Don't establish goals just to be able to say that you have some. If you do, you won't remain committed and motivated over time to attaining the goals. Write down only the things that you truly believe are pleasing to God or that come directly from God.

Take One Step at a Time

Goals are reached one step at a time. A certain amount of patience must accompany your persistence. Progress is sometimes slow, but if commitment, motivation, and desire remain steady, progress toward goals is evident. You may not have lost the ten pounds that you desired to lose before summer, but did you lose two pounds or five pounds? That's progress in the right direction! You may have missed a few days of reading your Bible, but did you read it twenty days last month? That's progress!

God has never been in a hurry. Jesus lived thirty long years on this earth before beginning His active public ministry. Was Jesus right on schedule? Was He fulfilling God's precise timetable? Yes!

Few things worth attaining can be accomplished in a day. What matters is the slow, steadfast, obedient pursuit of the goals to which God calls you. He is as concerned about your ongoing faithfulness, discipline, faith, obedience, and reliance upon Him as He is about your accomplishing the goals He helps you establish.

Set a Goal to Successfully Manage Your Success!

I encourage you to have the goal of successfully maintaining or managing the blessings that God sends your way. We each must be able to take responsibility for the goals we reach and for the blessings we receive.

A number of years ago, a man in our church made some brilliant financial moves and became very wealthy. Over a period of several months, the man's business claimed greater and greater amounts of his time and energy. His relationship with the church cooled. He once sat near the front of the church, eager to hear every word of a sermon. He gradually moved toward the back of the church and then up to the balcony. His attendance became sporadic.

The more he withdrew from the church and from pursuing his relationship with the Lord, the more he experienced problems in his business. The fact was, he didn't know how to handle or manage his success. Before long, he had lost most of the wealth he had acquired, and he was floundering spiritually.

It takes just as much wisdom and diligence to attain a goal as it does to maintain a goal that is reached.

Take the Plunge!

Do you remember the first time you stood at the edge of a swimming pool? One of your parents or perhaps a swimming instructor stood in the water and said, "Jump into my arms. I'm going to catch you. Come on, jump!"

You were scared. Would that person really catch you? Finally you said to yourself, even though you may not have realized what you were doing, *I'm going to take the risk. I'm going to jump and see what happens.*

If you had never taken that risk, you might still be limited to shallow wading pools, and in all likelihood, you'd have a fear of being in water above your knees. If you had been too fearful to get into the water, you would never have learned to swim.

In like manner, many people are too afraid to trust God to help them set goals for their lives. I encourage you to take the plunge and write down some goals today. I firmly believe that if you are willing to jump into the arms of God and trust Him with your life, you'll learn to walk with the Lord to greater heights and to greater satisfaction than you've ever dreamed possible. And you'll move more fully into the success that He desires and has planned for you.

5

A Personalized Pattern for Your Success

One of the greatest differences between the world's message about success and God's plan for success is this: the world seeks one formula that produces one set of results for all people. God's plan is far more creative. God establishes one set of principles and then seeks, by the power of His Holy Spirit, to manifest these principles according to each person's unique spiritual gifts, natural talents, personality, and circumstances and situations.

The Bible gives us many examples of people who were successful in a moment—perhaps in winning a battle or in an act that brought about the deliverance of the Israelites from an oppressive ruler. However, the entire lives of three men in the Bible portray distinct patterns of success. Each was successful in his own environment and generation, but in very different ways.

The Success Pattern of Joseph's Life

Joseph, the eleventh of twelve sons born to Jacob, was successful in God's eyes. God both planned and provided for his success.

As a youth, Joseph gained an understanding of God's personal success plan for him. He was given divine insight into God's plan for his future, which included prominence, power, and prestige. He knew for years and years—even though circumstances said otherwise—that God wanted to do something in his life and with his life.

Joseph's understanding of his future personal success was based upon two dreams God gave to him when he was only seventeen years old. At the time, Joseph's job was to feed his father's flocks. In one dream, however, Joseph was working not as a shepherd but as a grain gatherer. He and his brothers were binding sheaves in a field, and Joseph's sheaf arose while all of the other sheaves bowed down to his sheaf. In another dream, Joseph saw the sun, moon, and eleven stars bowing down to him.

Like many people today, Joseph had a dream of success, but no plan for success. God had given him a glimpse of his future, but had not provided any of the intervening details. It was up to Joseph to pursue God's plan for success with faith and obedience in doing the things that the Lord put in his path to do.

Many people are in the position that Joseph was in. They have a feeling or a knowing deep inside that their lives are supposed to count for something and that God has a purpose for their existence on the earth. They have dreams of success. But they don't know exactly how God is going to bring about their success.

As they look around at the circumstances surrounding their lives, they see no sign of success. Instead, they may see mounds of books that need to be read and studied, mounds of paperwork that must be shuffled to its next destination, or mounds of laundry that need to be moved from wash basket to washing machine.

They have the seed of a success dream buried indelibly in the heart and mind, but they do not see success unfolding around them. They have a feeling they are "on hold," just waiting for God to reveal His next step.

And what are they required to do while in this waiting phase? Be obedient to the tasks at hand.

A Daily Trust-and-Obey Relationship

God never asks any of us to sit down and wait idly for Him to vault us into success. He asks us to trust and obey Him day by day, day in and day out, by doing the things that He entrusts us to do. He asks us to learn the lessons that He sets before us—some of which may be painful, some of which may be difficult, and many of which may seem unimportant. Some of the work that God gives us to do may seem menial and totally unrelated to the end result of our success. Often we cannot see that God is building a strong pattern of experience, skill, trustworthiness, honesty, integrity, and character into us, so that when the time comes for us to be in a position of authority or influence, we will be ready.

Success May Be the Reality Even If Outcomes Initially Look Like Failures

Joseph had to pursue God's definition of success even when everything around him appeared to be headed for failure. Joseph was not being treated as number one when his father sent him to check on his brothers and the flocks in Shechem. Joseph was his father's errand boy at that point—a messenger, or in our terms today, a guy in the mailroom. He was at the bottom rung on the ladder, asked to do a task that any servant could have done for Jacob.

Was Joseph a success in his search for his brothers? Yes, but not entirely by his own ability. He found his brothers with a little help from a man he stopped to ask along the way.

Was Joseph a success when his brothers responded to his arrival by throwing him into a pit, intending to leave him for dead, and then later deciding to sell him as a slave to a passing band of Midianite traders? Yes. On what basis was he a success? He continued to trust God and to live as a person of honor and integrity. How do we know that was his response?

Because the Bible says he served Potiphar, an officer of Pharaoh and captain of the guard, in such an honorable way that Potiphar knew "the LORD was with Joseph, and he was a successful man" (Gen. 39:2). Potiphar took as a sign of Joseph's success that the Lord made "all he did to prosper in his hand" (Gen. 39:3).

Was Joseph a success when Potiphar's wife attempted to seduce him and Joseph refused her offers and ran from her presence, leaving his garment behind—an act that resulted in his being falsely accused and sent to a place where the king's prisoners were confined? Yes, Joseph was still a success. How do we know? Because Joseph continued to obey God in the prison, and the Lord "showed him mercy, and He gave him favor in the sight of the keeper of the prison" (Gen. 39:21). Joseph was put in charge of all the prisoners and had great authority in that prison "because the LORD was with him; and whatever he did, the LORD made it prosper" (Gen. 39:23).

Was Joseph a success when he interpreted the two dreams of Pharaoh's butler and baker? Yes. His interpretations of the dreams were right on target.

Was Joseph a success even though the butler forgot his promise to tell Pharaoh about Joseph for two long years? Yes. Joseph continued to trust God, and when the time came for Joseph to interpret Pharaoh's strange dream, he was ready. The Lord revealed to him the meaning of the dream, and in a day, Joseph went from being a prisoner to being the number-two man in Egypt. Pharaoh said to Joseph,

Inasmuch as God has shown you all this, there is no one as discerning and wise as you. You shall be over my house, and all my people shall be ruled according to your word; only in regard to the throne will I be greater than you . . . See, I have set you over all the land of Egypt. (Gen. 41:39–41)

Certainly Joseph may not have felt successful when he was on a journey into slavery in Egypt or when he was cast into Pharaoh's prison. But in

God's eyes, Joseph had not failed, and God's purposes for him were continuing to unfold. Later, when Joseph had an opportunity to provide again for his father and brothers and their families in a time of severe famine, Joseph concluded,

> God sent me before you to preserve a posterity for you in the earth, and to save your lives by a great deliverance. So now it was not you who sent me here, but God; and He has made me a father to Pharaoh, and lord of all his house, and a ruler throughout all the land of Egypt. (Gen. 45:7–8)

Joseph knew that the Lord had planned and provided for his success.

What is the general success pattern that we see in Joseph's life? It is a pattern of *vision* followed by years of *faithful preparation, trust,* and *obedience* resulting in years of *service, authority,* and *reward.*

We see this pattern in the lives of a number of Christian leaders through the centuries. Many men and women can say, "I had a dream when I was a child," or "God placed this on my heart when I was just a young teenager," or "I felt the call of God on my life when I was just a youngster." These same men and women spent years in training, studying, and preparing themselves, and perhaps even years of work and ministry—sometimes in very small churches, in out-of-the-way mission stations, in rural areas, in menial tasks for a ministry organization. And then the time came when God seemed to say, "You're ready now. I am moving you into the limelight. I am bringing you to the forefront. Now is the hour for which you have been prepared."

Trust, Obedience, and Faithful Preparation

Jesus spoke of this pattern of success in one of His parables. As you read through this familiar passage of Scripture, look for the elements of trust, obedience, and faithful preparation that were part of God's success plan:

[Jesus said,] "For the kingdom of heaven is like a man traveling to a far country, who called his own servants and delivered his goods to them. And to one he gave five talents, to another two, and to another one, to each according to his own ability; and immediately he went on a journey. Then he who had received the five talents went and traded with them, and made another five talents. And likewise he who had received two gained two more also. But he who had received one went and dug in the ground, and hid his lord's money. After a long time the lord of those servants came and settled accounts with them. So he who had received five talents came and brought five other talents, saying, 'Lord, you delivered to me five talents; look, I have gained five more talents besides them.' His lord said to him, 'Well done, good and faithful servant; you were faithful over a few things, I will make you ruler over many things. Enter into the joy of your lord.' He also who had received two talents came and said, 'Lord, you delivered to me two talents; look, I have gained two more talents besides them.' His lord said to him, 'Well done, good and faithful servant; you have been faithful over a few things, I will make you ruler over many things. Enter into the joy of your lord.'" (Matt. 25:14–23)

Has the Lord put you into His service and given you specific things over which He has asked you to be faithful and which He is expecting you to "invest" and "multiply"? Do you have a deep-seated vision for your life, perhaps something that you have never shared with another person but that has been with you for many years? Is this the success pattern that God seems to be unfolding in your life?

The Success Pattern of Moses' Life

Moses was a successful person in God's eyes. The pattern of his success was very different from that of Joseph, however. Joseph did not appear to have any direct, face-to-face communication with the Lord, which Moses had on a number of occasions. Joseph had a vision for success early in his life, which Moses apparently did not have.

Many people seem to be able to relate to Joseph. They have a dream for their lives, but bad breaks keep happening to them. Most people say about Moses, "Oh, he was different. Moses was chosen by God for a very special mission."

Yes, Moses was chosen by God and so was Joseph and so are you. You were no less chosen by God for the plans and purposes He has for your life than Moses and Joseph were chosen by God. God did not create you and then scratch His head and say, "Now I wonder what I can do with *this* person." No! God already had a plan and a purpose in mind for your life when He created you. He created you to *be* and to *do* very specific things in your lifetime.

"But," you may say, "Moses led a special life. He grew up in Pharaoh's house." The fact is, most of us would never want to trade places with Moses in order to live such a *special* life.

Moses was born with a death warrant on his head. Most of us have never had that special experience and never would want to have it. Moses' parents were under the order of Pharaoh to throw their baby son into the river. And that's precisely what Moses' mother did when Moses was just three months old—she threw him into the river in a boat. Pharaoh had neglected to say anything against throwing the babies into the river in little tar-lined baskets that were waterproof and could float!

Moses may have grown up in Pharaoh's court, but he grew up, for the most part, not knowing his immediate family, his relatives, or his Hebrew people. He was nursed by his own mother until he was weaned, but then he became a foster child of Pharaoh.

As an adult, Moses murdered an Egyptian who was abusing Hebrew workers. He spent the next forty years in fear as a fugitive on the run from Pharaoh. He went to Midian and married the daughter of a priest there. Again, he was separated from his family and his people. Most of us would never want such a special life. It was only after forty years of tending sheep that God called to Moses from a burning bush and revealed to him the success purpose of his life.

Did Moses know all along that he was a Hebrew? Yes, I believe he did. Did Moses know all along that God was going to use him or how God was going to use him? No, we have no indication of that in the Bible. When the Lord spoke to Moses from the burning bush, the Lord began by introducing Himself to Moses, saying, "I am the God of your father—the God of Abraham, the God of Isaac, and the God of Jacob" (Ex. 3:6). But when Moses heard that God wanted him to go back to the children of Israel and lead them out of Egypt, he said to the Lord, "Indeed, when I come to the children of Israel and say to them, 'The God of your fathers has sent me to you,' and they say to me, 'What is His name?' what shall I say to them?" And God said to Moses, "I AM WHO I AM" (Ex. 3:13–14).

Moses might not have known much about God at that point in his life, but God knew everything about Moses. He had been guiding Moses' life all along—just as He has been backstage and guiding your life all along.

God knew the day would come when He would need a man who was from the Hebrew family of Levi and raised with an intuitive understanding of God, but who would not have developed a mind-set as a slave. God knew He would need a man who had training in the ways of Egypt, who would know his way around Pharaoh's court, and who would be accepted and recognized as having a right to speak there, but who would not have been Egyptianized to the point of destroying his spirit or his sensitivity to the Hebrew people. God knew He would need a man who knew his way around wilderness areas and who knew how to lead a flock, but who also had leadership skills that could be employed in leading people.

You may not understand why God has given you the set of experiences you have had in your life. You may not see how they connect, much less where they are leading. You may not have any feeling at all that God has been guiding you, preparing you, preserving you, protecting you, or leading you all through your life to this moment.

I feel certain that when Moses looked back on his life, he could have concluded, "I was an abandoned baby, a foster child in a strange home, a murderer on the run from authorities at least half of my life, living in the desert with an alien group of people." Moses had no idea that his life was unfolding according to God's divine plan. But what about Moses from God's perspective? He was a man perfectly positioned for God's chosen success plan.

The same is true for you! God has a plan for your success that He is in the process of unfolding.

Trust God to Use Your Defeats

We would likely label as defeats some experiences of both Moses and Joseph. The fact is, every person has moments of defeat. No person lives without incidents that can be labeled as failures or setbacks. What about defeats? God has a way of weaving them into the success pattern of each person's life.

You may look back on things that seemed to be failures or defeats, and you say, "That experience made me stronger. It made me wiser. It made me more reliant upon God. It caused me to move into a new position, a new job, a new circle of friends, a new opportunity for ministry, or a new environment in which God could speak to me, use me, or develop in me things that were of great benefit to me later in my life."

Was Moses a success? Few people in the Bible are considered to be more successful. Moses led his people from slavery to freedom, from being "no people" to being "a people" with laws, customs, religious practices, and an identity among the nations. Moses brought the people into direct relationship with God and taught them to trust God for their daily provision of food and water, their daily guidance by a pillar of cloud or a pillar of fire, and to believe in God that a land of promise lay in their future.

Furthermore, Moses left a legacy of success to Joshua, who was his right-hand assistant for many years. He taught Joshua how to follow the Lord and lead the people simultaneously. He lived God's definition of success for his life and developed a *successor*—a person who would follow in his success footsteps.

What is the pattern of success we see in Moses? It perhaps can best be summarized this way: *seemingly unrelated events without vision* followed by a *call of God* (in which vision and events come together and make perfect sense) followed by *faithful obedience* and *trust* in pursuit of God's call.

A Similar Pattern in Paul's Life

In the New Testament, the apostle Paul seems to fit the Moses pattern. He spent his early years studying Torah and being the best Pharisee and Roman citizen he could possibly be. And then came his experience on the Damascus Road in which he surrendered his life to Christ. Suddenly Paul's life began to make sense. There was a reason he knew the Scriptures so well—he could see their fulfillment in Christ Jesus and teach the whole of God's message. There was a reason he was a Roman—he could travel unhindered and be protected by the Roman laws that pertained to freedom of speech and the right to a fair trial for Roman citizens.

For the rest of his days after his conversion to Christ, Paul followed the Lord with faithful obedience and absolute trust. He had a sharpened understanding about what the Lord had done in his life and about what his life had been before and after accepting Christ.

Many Christian men and women can attest to this pattern of success. They admit that they didn't think much about Jesus Christ or His plan for their success early in life. They just lived the days that unfolded before them. They took this job and that, married, had children, lived here and there, went to this church and that church on various occasions, and became involved with groups and projects and hobbies that happened to come along. But then one day, God got their attention. They surrendered their total lives to God and made a commitment to follow Him wherever He led them. And from that moment on, God manifested Himself in them and through them. He called them to specific tasks of ministry and blessed their obedience with specific miracles and insights into His Word. He revealed to them that He had been with them and working on their behalf all along. They could see how their past had prepared them for the future God held out to them. It was as if God pulled back the curtain on their past and showed them who they were in Him all along. And they began to walk in the fullness of God's success plan.

Is this the pattern that God seems to be unfolding or that He has revealed to you regarding your life?

The Success Pattern of King David's Life

A third pattern of success in the Bible is well represented by David, the youngest son of Jesse. David had a series of visible and outward successes, one building upon another and yet another.

As a boy watching his father's flocks, David was successful. He killed a bear and a lion while protecting the sheep entrusted to him. David said to King Saul,

> Your servant used to keep his father's sheep, and when a lion or a bear came and took a lamb out of the flock, I went out after it and struck it, and delivered the lamb from its mouth; and when it arose against me, I caught it by its beard, and struck and killed it. (1 Sam. 17:34–35)

As a young man visiting his brothers in the army that was cowering before the taunting threats of Goliath, David rose up to be successful. He faced Goliath—the warrior champion giant of the Philistines—and came away the winner. (See 1 Sam. 17:45–51.)

As the leader of Israel's armed forces, David was highly successful in battle, to the point that people cried, "Saul has slain his thousands, and David his ten thousands" (1 Sam. 18:5–7).

As a son-in-law of King Saul and a member of the court, David faced a new enemy—King Saul himself. And David was successful in side-stepping the javelins that Saul threw at him in jealousy. Again and again, he managed to escape the soldiers Saul sent to take him captive or to kill him.

As a king, David successfully ruled in Hebron for seven years and then took Jerusalem as his capital, taking over the governance of both the southern and the northern tribes of Israel. He successfully expanded and secured the borders of Israel and made all the necessary preparations for building the temple in Jerusalem.

As a king forced from his throne as the result of a coup led by his own son, David escaped and regrouped his forces and successfully retook the throne God had given to him. He was successful in naming Solomon as his successor.

Did David experience moments of failure and defeat? Were there moments when David made mistakes or was on the verge of mistakes? Most assuredly. He came close to a devastating failure of judgment in the way he planned to treat Nabal. He made serious errors in his relationship with Bathsheba and in the way he dealt with her husband, Uriah. He made serious parenting errors in the way he dealt with Amnon and Absalom. And David paid mightily for his mistakes.

Even so, all along the way, God redeemed David's failures and turned them into ingredients for future success because David confessed his sins, repented of them, and sought to follow God with a renewed heart for obedience. David never stopped trusting God, and he never stopped acknowledging God as the Source of his strength and the One who had given him the throne.

The pattern of David's success might be termed *anointing* followed by *success built upon success* with only periodic failures or setbacks. Any detours or mistakes along the way were quickly reversed so that the overall pattern of David's life was one of success built upon success.

You may be thinking, *Well, David and Joseph were a lot alike. Both of them had hard times in their lives, and both overcame them or lived through them by their faith and obedience.*

That is true. But in other ways, David and Joseph were very different. Joseph had two dreams that seemed to symbolize a successful future. There was no way, however, that Joseph could have concluded from those dreams at age seventeen, "I'm going to be prime minister of Egypt." David, on the other hand, had a very specific moment of anointing from the prophet Samuel. He knew his destiny was to be king over God's people. He knew he was God's anointed choice for the top leadership position in his nation.

Prior to being prime minister, Joseph spent most of his life in negative circumstances that suddenly were turned into a highly positive circumstance. David spent most of his days in generally positive circumstances that were punctuated by negative, and sometimes serious, situations. David's life as a shepherd was not a bad life. Much of his life as a soldier living in the court of King Saul was a good life. Even when David was on the run from Saul, he lived most of those years in relative peace and safety, and in a position of leadership in which he experienced adequate provision for himself and his followers (even living under the protection of a Philistine king for a period).

As king, David had mostly good years. For virtually all of his life, he lived in freedom, at least to a degree. He may not have been able to come into the presence of Saul, but he could roam the hills of Judea as he felt God leading him. The crises came, but they were like dark gashes against an overall pattern of success. Joseph's early years were mostly in slavery or bondage of some type; he had no personal freedom.

Peter's Life Was Similar to David's

Peter is a man in the New Testament who seems to have followed the David pattern for success. Peter was a successful fisherman when Jesus first met him—he had a booming business along the north shore of the Sea of Galilee.

Peter continued to enjoy success as a follower of Jesus. He was one of Jesus' inner circle, along with James and John, who witnessed the transfiguration of Jesus and were the only apostles present at certain miracles, such as the raising of Jairus's daughter from her deathbed. Peter was the apostle to whom Jesus spoke the most. Peter is the only apostle who walked on water, however briefly, and he is the apostle who proclaimed, "You are the Christ, the Son of the living God" (Matt. 16:16).

Yes, Peter had his failures. He made mistakes on occasion—including failure to use his faith in calming a storm and failure in cutting off the ear of the high priest's servant. Jesus rebuked him for failing to understand that Jesus would be crucified. He denied Jesus three times after Jesus' arrest. But those were incidents of which Peter quickly repented.

Peter preached a sermon on the day of pentecost that added three thousand members to the newly established church. Peter brought healing to a disabled man at the Beautiful Gate and raised Aeneas from a bed of paralysis and Dorcas from the dead. Peter opened the door to the Gentiles to receive Christ Jesus. Peter defended the rights of the gentile Christians to the Jews in Jerusalem. Peter taught mostly among the Jews of the early church, establishing them in the "way" of Jesus.

Peter went from success to success after Jesus initially said to him and his fishing partners, "Follow Me, and I will make you become fishers of men" (Mark 1:17).

This pattern illustrated in David's life and Peter's life can be found in a number of Christian men and women, not only in the past but also in the present. They are raised in godly homes, and they love the Lord all their lives. Their understanding of God and their relationship with God grow and mature over the years. When they experience failures or defeats, they turn to God and continue to trust God, they remain obedient to God to the best of their ability, and they seek to learn from their failures so that they don't repeat them. They grow and mature from strength to strength as God continues to refine them and use them in greater and greater ways.

Many pastors begin by pastoring small churches, then they are called to larger churches, and then to very large churches. Many Christian businessmen see their lives in this David pattern—they first established small businesses, but the businesses then grew and diversified over time, weathering hard periods and sometimes painful decisions.

Is this the success pattern that the Lord seems to be unfolding in your life?

A Unique Pattern for Each Person

In these biblical examples of success patterns we must recognize that God does not deal with any one of us precisely as He deals or has dealt with another person. We may want to be like David, only to realize that God has been dealing with us like Moses or Joseph. Even if God seems to have us on one of these three patterns, the exact circumstances and situations that He allows in our lives and the calls on our lives are unique.

You must never covet another person's success.

You must never discount what the Lord is doing in you or dismiss what the Lord desires to do through you.

You must never seek to define your success pattern in a way that is contrary to God's pattern.

To do so is to greatly hinder the work that God desires to do in you and to stall the fulfillment of God's plan for your success.

Your Response to God's Plan for Your Success

What, then, should be your response to the success pattern that God has designed uniquely for you?

First, you must continuously offer praise to God. You must continually praise the Lord for His work in your life. You must recognize with praise and thanksgiving that God has *always* been at work in you, and that He will continue to be at work in you—bringing you ultimately to wholeness and the perfection of His plan. Paul wrote, "Now may the God of peace Himself sanctify you completely; and may your whole spirit, soul, and body be preserved blameless at the coming of our Lord Jesus Christ. He who calls you is faithful, who also will do it" (1 Thess. 5:23–24).

Second, you must continue in the path God sets before you, regardless of setbacks, obstacles, or failures. You are called to endure hardship and to persevere in doing and saying the things that you know are right to do and say. You must persist in doing good as the Lord leads you.

It's easy to become discouraged if you don't receive recognition or the rewards that you believe should come your way. It's easy to think, *Nobody cares, including God.* It's easy to become dejected if others reject you or persecute you. The Lord never promised you that following Him would be easy. He promised that He would be with you and that His yoke upon your life would fit you, fulfill you, and give you the ability to be productive for the building of His kingdom if only you would do the work that He sets before you.

Third, you must encourage others to find and pursue the specific call that God has on their lives. No one walks the Christian journey alone. You are to be in fellowship with other believers—giving your strength to them in their times of weakness or discouragement, and receiving strength from them when you feel weak, tired, or disheartened. In encouraging others, your heart becomes encouraged.

God has a success plan for you. He designed it and built it into your life from the beginning. Your role is not to create your success, but to walk in the success path that He has already established for you.

6

PURSUING GOD'S GOALS FOR YOUR LIFE

If I drew a line in front of you today and I said, "Step over this line and your life will be better, beginning today," would you step over that line? I feel certain that there is a high degree of likelihood you would.

I give you that challenge today because I firmly believe that if you actually do what I tell you in this chapter and you begin to live out these principles drawn from God's Word, your life will be better, and you will be more successful, almost immediately, according to God's definition of *success*.

Doing Things God's Way

In the 1970s, a young man came to me in the church I was pastoring, and he said, "I'm going to be a success in life, and here's what I'm going to do." One principle on which he intended to base his success was that of OPM—Other People's Money. He showed me this principle in a book he was reading. I said to him, "You're reading the wrong thing. In the first place, you're defining success totally in terms of financial gain. And in the second place, you are seeking to *use* people rather than to earn an honest dollar for honest work. God won't honor either the intent of your heart or the methods you are seeking to employ."

In your pursuit of success, you must be committed to setting God's goals and then following through to fulfill God's goals in God's way.

God deals in terms of *what* and *who* and *how*. How you reach your goals is critical to being successful, not only in attaining the goals that God helps you set, but in developing the character that God wants you to develop in the process.

The principles for how to reach your God-given goals can be found in the story of David and Goliath (1 Sam. 17). I want to explore that story in depth with you.

Let me begin by giving you a little background about what was happening at the time of this confrontation between young David and the giant of the Philistines. The armies of the Philistines were camped on one side of the Valley of Elah and the armies of Israel were camped on the other side. This valley is fairly narrow. In fact, it is narrow enough for a person to shout across it and be heard. For forty consecutive days, Goliath had come out and stood in front of his army and shouted to the Israelites, "I defy the armies of Israel this day; give me a man, that we may fight together" (1 Sam. 17:10).

Goliath and the Philistines had set the terms for the battle. They wanted Saul to send out one soldier against Goliath. If the Israelite soldier prevailed in the battle, then the Philistines were willing to become the servants of Saul, but if Goliath prevailed, the Israelites would become the servants of the Philistines. A great deal was at stake.

The Israelites took one look at Goliath, and they were gripped by fear. Day after day, they failed to respond to Goliath's challenge.

Now, taking a look at the surface level of the situation, the Israelites had good cause to be afraid. Goliath was a champion of the Philistines. He was like an Olympic gold-medal winner. He had succeeded in defeating all of the other Philistines in hand-to-hand combat. He was the best of their best. And he was also among the biggest of their big.

Most historians state that a cubit was twenty-five inches (the length from the tip of the nose to the tip of the middle finger when the arm is outstretched), and a span was ten inches (the length from the tip of the thumb to the tip of the little finger when the fingers are stretched apart). Goliath was six cubits and a span tall—that calculates to thirteen feet, four inches! He truly was a giant.

He had a coat of bronze armor, a bronze helmet, and a spear that was like a weaver's beam, with a spearhead that weighed more than twenty-three pounds. His shield-bearer went before him carrying a shield that covered Goliath from neck to toe. The form of fighting that he was advocating was "thrust and retreat" from side to side around the shield. Goliath was superbly skilled in this type of fighting, using this type of armor.

For forty days, the Israelites had cowered in silence on their side of the valley, becoming increasingly demoralized as each day went by.

Meanwhile, Jesse had sent three sons to fight with Saul. When they didn't return in a timely manner, Jesse sent David, the youngest of his eight sons, to take food to the army and to see what was happening in the battle. David arrived on the scene, gave the food to the supply keeper, ran to the soldiers, and found his brothers. As he was talking to them, Goliath came out to issue his daily challenge. David heard him speak, and he quickly noted that all of the men of Israel were dreadfully afraid at the sight of this giant.

David immediately established what he believed with his whole heart was a goal that God desired to be accomplished. As we examine the rest of the story, I want you to see ten aspects of goal setting evident within it. Each one applies to your life and is vital to achieving your God-given goals.

1. A Clear Picture of the Goal

Any goal that you establish must be clear enough to state in a concise and meaningful manner. David had such a goal: "Kill Goliath."

Upon hearing Goliath's challenge, David asked, "What shall be done for the man who kills this Philistine and takes away the reproach from Israel? For who is this uncircumcised Philistine, that he should defy the armies of the living God?" (1 Sam. 17:26).

I want you to note two things about these questions. First, David had already perceived that Goliath must be defeated. He didn't ask, "Is it possible to defeat this guy?" He believed it could be done and needed to be done.

Second, David did not see Goliath as simply a champion soldier in search of a fight. He saw Goliath as an enemy of God. He called him an "uncircumcised Philistine" standing in defiance of the armies of the living God. David sought to kill Goliath not to achieve fame, but to remove the reproach that Goliath was bringing upon God's people. His goal was firmly rooted in God's greater goal for him.

You see, David had already been anointed to be the next king of Israel. Samuel had already been to his home and poured out the oil over David, and the Spirit of the Lord had come upon David. David was acting like the future king he would be. He had a heart for God's people and for establishing righteousness among the Israelites. Goliath was a threat to his people, his future subjects, his future reign. His desire to kill Goliath was not an act of violence or a desire for bloodshed—it was rooted in a desire to see God's people be free of an evil and oppressive enemy.

The Israelite soldiers responded to David that the person who killed Goliath would be given the king's daughter as a wife, great riches, and freedom from paying taxes. Those were not David's incentives for fighting Goliath, however. They were not good enough incentives for any of the other soldiers to desire to face Goliath! David's motivation was not the reward that might come from the king, but the reward that David knew would come from the King of kings, the sovereign King, the almighty God.

David's immediate goal—to kill Goliath—was only a facet of his much greater long-range goal to be a good king over all Israel one day. No enemy was worthy to stand before the God that David sought to serve with his whole heart.

Are your immediate goals clear and concise?

Are they relevant and important aspects of reaching your long-range goals and your priority goal to know Christ intimately and to be conformed to Christ's character?

Are your immediate goals part of the big goals that God has helped you to set?

2. A Consuming Desire to Reach Your Goal

A godly goal worth pursuing is not a goal that you can be talked out of. It is a goal that resides deep within you and that cannot be quenched by circumstances or by what others may say. A godly goal is a part of your becoming the person God desires for you to be. It is much more than simply doing something in the near future.

David had a consuming desire to accomplish his goal of killing Goliath. He had an abiding feeling deep within that this situation couldn't go on for another day, much less forty, sixty, or a hundred days. Something had to be done quickly. David had a burning passion and motivation for getting the job done *now*.

Any goal that is truly of God is going to have a fervency about it. The person is going to believe that the stakes are high—if the goal is not met, souls will be lost, and important things will not be accomplished in the course of God's plan for humanity. Godly goals have a built-in urgency about them, a passion that mirrors the passionate heart of God.

If God seems silent about your goal, then in all likelihood, it is not a goal He has helped you to set. On the other hand, if your mind and heart can hardly seem to contain all that might pertain to your goal—to the point that you can think of few other things and the pursuit of your goal is your first waking thought and the last thought before you fall asleep at night—it may very well be a passionate goal that God has placed in your heart.

When David heard Goliath challenge the Israelites, everything within him rose to the occasion. He could not walk away, and he could not allow the situation to continue. Everything inside him moved toward a solution to the problem.

Even when his older brothers tried to talk sense into him, David replied, "What have I done now? Is there not a cause?" (1 Sam. 17:29). David could not be dissuaded.

The degree of a person's commitment toward the pursuit of a goal will always be evidenced by a deep urgency, passion, enthusiasm, motivation, and excitement toward reaching that goal. For nearly two years, I had planned a photography trip to Switzerland. As the time drew close for my departure, did I say to myself and others, "Well, I'm off to Switzerland. I hope I have a good time"? No! I was eager to get there. I could hardly wait to get there. I had everything in place to take the photographs that I had dreamed of taking for two years. I was ready to go!

Do you have a goal today that is challenging you deep in your spirit? Do you have something that you are so motivated toward doing that you refuse to let any obstacle stand in your way? Are you excited about accomplishing your goals?

3. Confidence That You Will Reach Your Goal

David had no doubt whatsoever that he would be able to kill Goliath. He boldly said to King Saul, "Let no man's heart fail because of him; your servant will go and fight with this Philistine" (1 Sam. 17:32).

King Saul also tried to dissuade David, saying, "You are not able to go against this Philistine to fight with him; for you are a youth, and he a man of war from his youth" (v. 33).

David responded by telling King Saul about the lion and the bear he had killed, and he concluded, "This uncircumcised Philistine will be like one of them, seeing he has defied the armies of the living God" (v. 36).

David had awesome, overwhelming confidence, but it wasn't confidence only in his ability. He said, "The LORD, who delivered me from the paw of the lion and from the paw of the bear, He will deliver me from the hand of this Philistine" (v. 37).

Your confidence in reaching your God-given goal rests not in your ability or desire alone, but in the God who gave you the goal and the consuming desire to reach it in the first place.

As David rushed down the mountainside toward Goliath, he cried,

You come to me with a sword, with a spear, and with a javelin. But I come to you in the name of the LORD of hosts, the God of the armies of Israel, whom you have defied. This day the LORD will deliver you into my hand, and I will strike you and take your head from you . . . that all the earth may know that there is a God in Israel. Then all this assembly shall know that the LORD does not save with sword and spear; for the battle is the LORD's, and He will give you into our hands. (1 Sam. 17:45–47)

Talk about confidence! David was approaching a man more than twice his size, a recognized champion of an entire nation of warriors, a skilled soldier fully armed in bronze from head to toe, standing with a full-body shield in front of him. And still David said, "I will give your body and the carcasses of your fellow Philistines to the birds of the air and the wild beasts of the earth." (See 1 Sam. 17:46.)

David's confidence was related directly to his relationship with God and to his understanding that God would help him accomplish the goals that God had placed in his heart.

Your confidence in pursuing a God-given goal must be rooted in the same things: your relationship with God and your fervent belief that God has called you to succeed at the goals He has placed in your heart.

If you do not have confidence that you can reach the goal God has given you, you will not throw all of your energy into that effort, and you will easily become discouraged at the slightest obstacle or setback. Confidence in the Lord fuels motivation. It is the foundation for courage and endurance.

The apostle Paul had this same confidence. He wrote to the Philippians, "I can do all things through Christ who strengthens me" (Phil. 4:13). Even though he was writing from a prison cell, chained to a Roman soldier, Paul had an unshakable, inner confidence that he could do *all* things Christ was calling him to do.

Too many people allow themselves to become disheartened in the pursuit of their God-given goals. They say, "I must have heard God incorrectly. There surely must be someone else who is better suited for this goal. I'm just not up to the challenge."

You should ask, "Is God capable of doing this?" The answer must always be yes. God is capable of all things. The truth is, you *can't* do anything of lasting benefit on your own strength. The equal truth is, God hasn't asked you to do things of eternal benefit on your own. He has promised to be with you every step of the way and to work in you and through you to the accomplishing of His purposes. You *can* do all things He calls you to do because He is at work in you to do them!

Egotism is based on self-strength. It is having confidence in one's own abilities. And for that reason, egotism is ultimately an expression of false confidence. Genuine confidence is to be found only when you place your trust in God and rely on Him to get a job done.

Through the years, I have encountered a number of people who believe they have God-given goals but then say, "I hope I can do it." My word to them is, "Forget this 'hope' business. Don't say, 'I hope I can.' Say, 'I'm going to do this because God has set this goal, I'm going to give it all I've got, and I'm trusting God to accomplish this goal in His way, in His timing, and for His glory.'" Don't *hope* that you'll succeed. *Expect* to succeed.

4. A Course of Action

For any goal to be met, a course of action must be taken. A decision must be made to do something, and steps must be put into motion toward getting the job done.

Most goals cannot be reached in one moment or with one act. Most major goals—most long-term goals and certainly goals that are lifelong, priority goals with eternal consequences—require a sequence of steps for them to be accomplished.

What was David's course of action? First, David knew that he needed Saul's approval. He couldn't go rushing down the mountainside at Goliath on his own strength. Given the fear of the Israelites, he likely would have been speared in the back if he had tried that. They would not have wanted Goliath to think that he was the one they were sending out because they knew that the penalty for defeat was being in servitude to the Philistines from that day onward. No—David required official approval to face off with Goliath. David first had to go to Saul to convince Saul that he could get the job done. He needed Saul to say, "Go, and the LORD be with you!" (1 Sam. 17:37).

Next, David had to deal with the matter of armor. Saul offered David his own armor, but the minute David put it on, he knew it wouldn't work. We read in 1 Samuel 17:39, "David fastened his sword to his armor and tried to walk . . . And David said to Saul, 'I cannot walk with these, for I have not tested them.'" David couldn't operate with the traditional coat of armor.

Next, David pursued the method that he believed would work for him. He went down to the creek with his staff in his hand, chose five smooth stones, and put them in his shepherd's bag. He didn't rely upon anyone else to choose his stones. David knew from his experience in fending off wild animals from his father's flocks which stones would fly through the air fastest and straight toward the target.

And it was only then—after getting Saul's approval to fight, getting

Saul's approval to fight *in the way David wanted to fight*, and choosing his own weapons—that David "drew near" to the Philistine Goliath.

Goliath saw him coming and laughed. He said, "Am I a dog, that you come to me with sticks?" And then he cursed David and threatened him. (See 1 Sam. 17:43–44.)

David wasn't the least bit upset by what Goliath did. It was almost as if he had planned it that way. You can almost hear David thinking, *Let him totally underestimate me. Let him ridicule me rather than take me seriously. He doesn't know he is underestimating the Lord God!*

All that David did put Goliath off guard. Overconfident and not fully alert to what was happening, Goliath lumbered out toward David, roaring threats at each step. David, for his part, shouted back. He refused to be intimidated by Goliath. From David's perspective, Goliath should have been intimidated by him! He came at Goliath running and shouting and all the while reaching into his bag, taking out a stone, putting that stone in his slingshot, and whirling that slingshot until he let go of the stone straight for the one little patch above Goliath's eyes that was not covered with bronze. His aim was perfect.

Once you have written down goals in various areas of your life, you are only at the beginning of accomplishing the goals. You must now turn the goals into a course of action—a set of steps, a mapped-out plan, a strategy for getting the job done. Goals must be turned into plans, and plans must then be worked. You can have the finest and most challenging goal possible, but if you don't turn that into a course of action and take action to implement your plan, your goal will remain just that—a goal.

Consider the goal of going on a family mission trip. You have a strong desire to serve the Lord together as a family in a place of need. You have a clear goal about what you want to accomplish, you have a burning desire to take the trip, and you have confidence that you are going to be able to go on a mission trip and successfully do what you dream of doing. But what next? You must turn that goal into a workable plan.

You need to save money for the trip. You need to spend time with your family members talking about the trip and determining where to go and why. You need to contact an organization that arranges for such trips or contact a missionary to see if you can be of service. You need to get passports and perhaps visas and immunizations if you are going to certain parts of the world. You need to arrange for time off from work and for the care of your house and perhaps your pets and yard. Many details need attention for you to fulfill your goal of taking a family mission trip. You need a course of action.

What are you doing today to turn your goal into a reality? Do you have a plan, a strategy, a sequence of steps that must be taken?

5. A Calendar of Events

You must put the steps of your course of action on a timetable. It's not enough to say, "One of these days I'm going to buy a car," or "Someday I'll get around to redecorating the house." Any person who has these goals knows that "one of these days" is often "none of these days" and "someday" often is elusive. To be wise in the purchase of a new car, you are going to have to visit car dealerships to see how much the automobile of your choice costs and what kind of payment plans are available. You are going to have to map out a savings plan so that you have sufficient money to buy a car or at least make a substantial down payment.

Many people in our nation do not have wills when they die. They intend to take care of this matter and have intended to do so for years. For countless reasons, they never get around to it. A legal will doesn't just happen. It takes calling and setting up a meeting with an attorney.

It's amazing what happens when you put a date next to a goal. Things seem to begin to move. Your conscious and subconscious mind go to work on the task. You move the goal from the "idea" stage to the "reality" stage.

If a project team at work has only thirty days to complete a project, things are put into motion pretty quickly. If the boss says only "as soon as possible" or "when you get around to it," virtually nothing happens.

We need to become acutely aware that we have only one life in which to serve the Lord on this earth. What we're going to accomplish, we need to be accomplishing *now*. We can't reclaim the time we lost yesterday or the time we squandered last week. Today is the day for action.

David had an *immediate* timetable for taking on Goliath. He didn't say, "Well, now that I have Saul's approval to fight, I'm going to sit back and wait a while." No! He went into action immediately. He didn't give anybody an opportunity to talk him out of the battle, including his brothers. He didn't give them time to send a message home to their father, Jesse. He didn't give himself time to second-guess or to try to overanalyze what he knew deep within needed to be done and needed to be done *now*. He didn't wait for dark so that if he failed, nobody would notice. David took action!

6. Cooperation of Others

On the surface, the story of David facing Goliath may seem like a one-man show. That is hardly the case, however. David's ultimate intent was not merely to kill Goliath but to destroy the entire Philistine army that had come against the Israelites. Destruction of the whole army was his secondary goal, one he stated to Goliath when he said, "This day I will give the carcasses of the camp of the Philistines to the birds of the air and the wild beasts of the earth" (1 Sam. 17:46).

David could not take on the whole army by himself. And in the end, he did not take on anyone but Goliath that day. After the stone from David's slingshot penetrated Goliath's forehead and he fell on his face to the earth, David rushed toward Goliath, pulled the sword from Goliath's sheath, and cut off Goliath's head. Both the Philistines and the Israelites knew with certainty that Goliath was dead.

The Philistines fled. The men of Israel and Judah arose and shouted and pursued the Philistines to the entrance of the valley and the gates of Ekron, wounding and killing many and plundering the tents of the goods left behind. The army of the Israelites routed the army of the Philistines after David killed the Philistine champion.

David had already spread word through the Israelite camp that they should be stirred up and ready to fight the Philistines. He said to his brothers, "Is there not a cause?" and the Bible tells us, "He turned from him [his brother] and said the same thing" to everybody who would hear him. It was David's repeated and insistent questioning, "Is there not a cause to fight this giant Goliath?" that brought David to King Saul's attention. David was already rallying the troops for the battle that would lie ahead. David was fully confident that he was going to kill Goliath—he needed the rest of the army to be ready to undertake the battle against the rest of the Philistine army after he had done his part.

No goal that God gives to an individual is set in isolation. God deals with His people. He may single out a man or a woman to lead a particular task or to be the rallying point for a particular cause or project, but in the end, God desires that many people be involved in the goals that He gives to us. He expects us to cooperate as the body of Christ and to learn to love one another in the process of functioning as the family of God.

In what ways does the Lord expect you to involve others in the goals He has helped you set? What steps are you taking to include others, to inspire others, to share the joy of pursuing your goal with others?

Earlier, I mentioned that I do not believe it is wise to publish widely the long-range goals that God gives you. At some point, however, it is generally wise to tell others about an immediate or short-range step toward reaching a goal. You do not need to spell out the entire goal or chart out all of the remaining steps toward it.

Most people cannot commit to assisting someone with more than an immediate goal or challenge. Furthermore, the goal must be one they are convinced is achievable and toward which they believe they can make a significant contribution of time, energy, resources, prayer, or some other form of assistance. Rally cooperation for short segments of time and for specific and readily measurable and doable tasks.

Certainly a person can do a few things on his own, but these goals are rarely major ones. When I think about all of the various programs and opportunities for ministry connected with a large church, I am acutely aware that these programs do not happen through the efforts of only one person. A choir, an orchestra, a drama department, a Sunday school program, a mission program, television and radio outreaches, the production of publications, an annual church picnic or dinner, an active correspondence ministry, a vibrant youth department, an active singles ministry, a small group Bible study, and even a church service involve many people, most of whom work behind the scenes.

The same is true for the major projects you face as a family, a community, or a social or service organization.

The good news is that if the Lord has truly laid the goal on your heart, He is already at work preparing the hearts of others to help you reach the goal. To a degree, He has imparted the same goal or desire to their hearts. Most people are willing to help another person reach a goal if they are shown the goal's importance to the plan and purposes of God.

For the most part, other people aren't all that excited about the full range of *your* goals. They are much more excited about *their* goals. Only as people see that their goals are in sync with your goals will they choose to help you.

When you set family goals, you must share your goals with your spouse and be in full agreement about the things involving your whole family. It is also important to share certain goals with your children at as early an age as you believe it is wise for them to have the information. Family goals require family cooperation.

When everyone in a family or an organization is informed and involved in the pursuit of a goal, added energy and enthusiasm build momentum toward reaching the goal. When the fruit of the goal becomes a reality, the entire group has opportunity to rejoice. Reaching short-range goals is motivating and builds faith, furthering the pursuit of long-range goals.

7. Consistency in the Pursuit of Goals

Once you have set your eyes on a goal, do not allow yourself to be pulled off course. If you truly believe God has helped you set a goal, do not allow anyone to deter you, stall you, or hinder you as you pursue it.

There may be occasions when others can help you clarify your goal, or others may offer wise advice about how to reach a goal more efficiently and effectively. Weigh all advice carefully, and above all, ask God to confirm whether you should follow the advice. Always remember that King Saul offered David his armor, the most excellent armor in all the army, but that armor wasn't right for David. The ideas of others may not be the ideas that God wants you to follow. In other cases, God may use a person to give you the very idea, solution, or answer He knows you need.

As you pursue your goals, you must keep one eye on your long-range goals, even as you throw your energies into accomplishing the immediate or short-range goals connected to it.

Consistency Until the Goal Is Fully Reached. Follow-through is vital. David didn't strike Goliath with a stone from his slingshot and then leap about in wild enthusiasm that the giant was on the ground. To the contrary, he moved ahead and made certain that Goliath was dead. And in case anybody was likely to discount or to diminish the importance of what David had done that day on behalf of Israel, he brought Goliath's head back to Jerusalem as proof that God had delivered His people from their enemy.

Consistency Over Time. You reach goals more quickly if you are consistent over time in their pursuit.

When it comes to family goals, one of the greatest attributes you can display to your children is consistency over time. Your children do not need to hear from you only once that God loves them and that you love them. They need to hear that message every day of their lives. They need to be tucked into bed each and every night with the message, "God loves you and I love you."

Your children do not need to hear Bible stories just once or attend church just once a year or attend Sunday school for just a month. They need to hear Bible stories again and again, attend church every week, and be involved in Sunday school every week. They need to hear you read Bible stories, and they need to hear others tell Bible stories and expound on them—the more they hear the truth of the Bible and the more voices they hear confirming the same truth, the more they are going to come to believe what the Bible says.

You need to explain to your child *how* to receive Jesus as Savior. You need to pray daily with your child so that your child learns how to communicate with God. You need to tell your child week after week that God has a plan for his life. Help your child discover God's goals for his own life. Encourage your child to think about the plans that God may have for his future.

Do these things again and again and again. Training a child means instilling and reinforcing and repeating principles and the behaviors that you want your child to call his own.

Consistency and Commitment. The consistency with which you pursue your God-given goals is directly related to the degree of your commitment to obeying God and doing what God is leading you to do. How important is it today that you reach the goals God has laid on your heart and implanted into your very spirit? How committed are you to doing what God has said? If you are committed only in a halfhearted way, you won't be very consistent. If you are deeply committed and eager to obey God and reach the goals God has led you to set, then you are going to be consistent.

Every morning when I awake, one thought prevails: *What can I do today that will enable me to at least partially, to some degree, move toward reaching my goal of getting the gospel to every nation on the face of this earth as quickly as possible, as simply as possible, as clearly as possible, and as irresistibly as possible, by the power of the Holy Spirit and to the glory of God?* As I set my daily agenda and make decisions about how to use my time, resources, and energy in a given day, that question is always there. And the result is that I have a consistency about what I do and don't do. Some things obviously become unimportant or unnecessary. Other things become vital and urgent.

If something isn't worthy of your concentration and your consistency, it probably isn't worthy to be called a God-given goal.

8. Controlling Your Emotions

As you pursue a God-given goal, you will have many opportunities to become frustrated and perhaps even angry. Don't give full sway to those emotions. Keep your emotions under control as you press toward your goal. Negative emotions can not only deter you from taking necessary forward-motion action or put you on a detour away from a task or project; they can sap your energy and put you into a state of exhaustion, discouragement, and even depression.

David had several opportunities to become frustrated or angry when he went to the battle site that day. He could have become involved in a major argument with his brothers or the other soldiers. He could have turned and gone home in frustration, with feelings of rejection. David could have become angry with King Saul for saying to him, "You are not able to go against this Philistine" (1 Sam. 17:33). However, David saved all of his emotional energy for the battle.

As you pursue a God-given goal, you are going to have to make a decision that you will save your emotional energy for the moments, decisions, and actions that are truly important to reaching your goal. There are lots of things that can, and must, be overlooked or not blown out of proportion. There are lots of little differences and petty arguments that need to be sidestepped. There are lots of personality quirks and unimportant matters of personal style that need to be ignored. Stay focused on what is truly important to God.

Some people allow criticism and rejection to bog them down. They get caught up in what someone says or the look on a person's face or the turn of a person's shoulder. Those who allow these actions to deter them from their God-given purpose in life are more concerned about a person's acceptance than about God's acceptance and love.

Determine within yourself that you are going to keep your focus on God's love, God's call, God's help, God's approval, God's rewards. He will not disappoint you, fail you, reject you, or criticize the things that you do with a heart of love and a desire to obey.

Now I certainly am not advocating that you overlook matters of sin, evil, or rebellion against God. Those things need to be nipped in the bud at their earliest appearance. But you need to ignore individual differences and moments when things are said carelessly. These issues should not be blown out of proportion. As someone said, "Some molehills should just remain molehills."

Take charge over fear. Have you ever stopped to think that David was very likely afraid as he rushed down toward Goliath? I believe he was afraid to a degree. He knew he was facing a life-and-death struggle. Only one man was going to come out of that valley alive—Goliath or David. And while David believed with all of his heart, mind, and soul that he was going to be the victor because God was with him, David nonetheless was aware of the importance of the battle. He wasn't in denial. He wasn't blindly and egotistically taking on the giant. He knew fully what was at stake. And there was no skirting the issue that it was a fearful situation.

We know from his behavior, however, that David did not let fear paralyze him. He used the emotions associated with fear to fuel his faith into an even greater blaze.

You and I are challenged to do the same. At times we may be fearful in pursuit of a goal. The challenge we face is to rule our fear rather than allow our fear to rule us. We must not let fear stop us or slow us down. We must speak faith to our hearts so that as much as we may feel fear, we feel faith a hundred times more potent stirring in us.

A musical performer or actor will tell you that no matter how many times he has performed onstage, he still feels butterflies before a performance. The professional uses that inner stirring, that inner energy, to make his performance even more potent. We are called to do the same. We must rule our fear, take charge of it, and turn it into a statement and an act of faith.

Encourage others and yourself. One of the most important and beneficial things you can do as you pursue a God-given goal is to encourage yourself often, even as you encourage those who may be helping you or working in close proximity to you. We all respond to encouragement and praise more than we respond to criticism. Show me a child who hears nothing but "You can't," "You shouldn't," "You won't ever," and "You are failing," and I will show you a child who is discouraged and who eventually will have no desire to face a challenge, take a risk, or pursue a goal.

On the other hand, show me a child who frequently hears "I believe in you," "You can do this," "You're going to make it," "Don't give up—you're on your way," "'Atta boy," and I'll show you a child who has strong self-esteem, a much greater likelihood of trusting God in every area of his life, and a child who has great enthusiasm for taking on a new challenge or setting a new goal.

Be an encourager. Don't be a defeatist.

Watch what you say to yourself. Don't call yourself names. Don't be overly hard on yourself at each mistake you make or failure you experience. Speak positive, encouraging words to yourself. The Lord desires this for you. He doesn't come at you again and again with criticism. He desires for you to learn from your mistakes, pick yourself up, forgive yourself even as you seek His forgiveness, and walk forward in strength, courage, and trust.

9. Courage to Act

David obviously possessed extraordinary courage. It was not courage that he suddenly acquired on the day he faced Goliath, however. David had developed courage over a number of years and through a variety of circumstances.

It had taken courage for David to face a lion and a bear in his protection of his father's flocks. It had taken courage for David to stand up to his older brothers, and it had taken courage for David to meet with the king of the Israelites.

Very few of us find ourselves in situations that call for immediate and extraordinary courage. Yet most of us have abundant opportunities to develop courage over time, by standing up for what is right and by stating our case and acting in righteousness countless times, in countless ways, in the face of countless circumstances.

Ask the Lord today to give you daily courage to face the tasks He puts before you. Ask Him to give you courage to accomplish the immediate and short-range goals you have set.

One of the best ways I know to acquire courage is to read the Word of God and see how God has helped others through their difficulties, trials, and problems. Then get on your knees and ask God to give you the direction, guidance, and courage you need.

You will also benefit by associating with people who are encouragers. Choose to develop friendships and working relationships with people who are realistic about life, yet positive when it comes to overcoming obstacles. Choose to be around those who are energetic and enthusiastic about life and who aren't afraid to take risks and tackle tough problems.

I faced a great struggle when I first became senior pastor at the First Baptist Church in Atlanta. I seemed to meet daily opposition from a faction of the church that wanted to see me move elsewhere. At times, the internal pressure was intense.

From the "outside," I received letters from other churches asking me to consider becoming their senior pastor. Some of the requests had an urgent tone about them, and they represented a certain amount of external pressure.

I kept a stack of those letters on my desk—no doubt thinking, subconsciously, that I'd keep them handy just in case.

At the same time, I had the absolute confidence and assurance from the Lord that He had called me to be the senior pastor of the First Baptist Church in Atlanta. I had an inner motivation and knowing that God was with me in my work in Atlanta and that He had set the goal before me to be the pastor of this particular congregation.

Every day, I would go to the prayer room at the church until I had absolute reassurance that I was walking in the perfect center of God's will for my life. But then I'd leave the prayer room, and *wham*, I'd encounter a challenge to my faith and confidence.

I was in South Carolina preaching a revival. A fellow pastor, who was significantly older than I, handed me a little paperback book and said, "Charles, I want you to read this book I'm giving you." I took his words as serious fatherly advice.

When I got back to Atlanta, I began to read the book and couldn't put it down. One particular idea in the book burned itself into my mind: "When a man is willing to burn every bridge behind him and cut every rope of escape and move toward his goal, he cannot lose." I read and reread that statement. And then I went to my desk, gathered up all of the letters offering me other positions, and threw them into the trash. I made a new commitment of resolve that I would not be budged from God's plan for my life and for First Baptist in Atlanta until God moved me. I've been the senior pastor of this church for almost thirty years.

Those letters offering me other positions had created for me a divided mind. They had kept me thinking, *What if?* They had provided a distraction. When I swept those offers aside and set myself to fulfill the challenge God had placed before me, I felt not only new resolve, but also new courage. I came to the point where I *chose to do what I had to do*. And friend, that's what courage is all about. It's choosing with your will to follow through and do what you have to do in order to be in full obedience to God's goals for your life.

There are times when we need to burn the bridges to our past and cut the ropes that tie us to things in which we place our security. There are times when we have to fling ourselves on the faithfulness of God. It takes courage to do so.

10. A Conscious Dependence on God

When you read 1 Samuel 17 as a whole, you will find that David repeatedly referred to the Lord. He told King Saul, "The LORD is the one who delivered me from the paw of the lion and the paw of the bear." He told Goliath, "I come to you in the name of the LORD of hosts. The LORD will deliver you into my hand. This assembly shall know that the LORD does not save with sword and spear. The battle is the LORD's. The LORD will give you into our hands." David had a conscious, openly expressed dependence on God.

God desires that you depend on Him. You are not a burden on God when you say to Him, "My absolute, total dependence is on You." God desires that you have an attitude of utter and complete reliance upon Him.

Not only are you to have an attitude of dependence upon the Lord, but your conversation and your statements to others should reflect this dependence. You cannot accomplish anything of eternal benefit on your own strength. You must remind yourself and others by what you say that the things of eternal benefit require you to trust God to work out *His* purposes in your life and in the lives of others.

7

WHAT ABOUT MONEY?

A pervasive deception in our nation today is that success equals wealth. The truth is, becoming the person God wants you to be and achieving the goals He sets for your life make you successful.

Wealth has virtually nothing to do with your becoming the person God wants you to be. And wealth, solely for the sake of acquiring wealth, is not a goal that God sets for anyone's life. You will find no admonition of God in the Scriptures for you to seek and strive to become rich materially.

Does this mean that a rich person is not successful in God's eyes?

Does it mean that God never blesses a person with material wealth or with nice possessions?

No.

It means that wealth is not the gauge by which we should determine a person's success. God has an entirely different standard and means of measurement.

Back in 1923, six of the wealthiest men in our nation met in a hotel in Chicago. They had been exceedingly wealthy for years, and they were often proclaimed in the media as good role models for children to follow.

Who were these six men? Let me name them and tell you what happened to them. And then you decide if they were truly successful in their lives:

1. Charles Schwab, president of the largest independent steel company at the time. He lived on borrowed money the last five years of his life and died penniless.

2. Richard Whitney, president of the New York Stock Exchange. He served time in Sing-Sing prison at the end of his life.

3. Albert Fall, a member of the president's cabinet. He was pardoned from prison at the end of his life so he could go home to die.

4. Jesse Livermore, the greatest bear on Wall Street. He committed suicide.

5. Ivan Krueger, head of the world's greatest monopoly at the time. He also committed suicide.

6. Leon Frasier, president of the Bank of International Settlement. He, too, committed suicide.

The combined resources of these six men at one time equaled more than the funds in the entire United States Treasury.

Wealthy? Yes. They were wealthy beyond the wildest imaginations of most of us. But were they successful? No.

God is never impressed by monetary wealth. He is impressed by our obedience, our faith, and our reliance upon Him to guide us in all matters.

Consider the godly mother who is raising her three children the best she knows how—working a nine-to-five shift to support herself and her children because her husband has abandoned her. She reads Bible stories to her children every night and kneels down by their beds to pray with them. She would rather take her children to the park on Saturday and to church on Sunday than work overtime or a second shift.

Will this woman become a wealthy person? Probably not.

Will she be blessed in the eyes of the Lord? I have no doubt she will. She will have the joy and contentment of the Lord in her heart, knowing that she has been the best mother she could possibly be. She'll have the reward of seeing her children grow up to serve God and honor her all the days of their lives. She'll have a lasting, eternal blessing of living forever with her children in heaven. Rich? Oh, yes, beyond measure. But not in terms of dollars and cents on this earth.

Consider the man who spends eighty hours a week in his corporate high-rise office, with only time out once a week for a round of golf with his business associates. He rarely sees his wife and children, and he rarely attends his son's games or his daughter's recitals. He goes to church only on Christmas and Easter and only then because nobody else is at work and the financial markets are closed.

Will this man become wealthy? There is a great possibility that he will. Will this man be blessed in God's eyes? I doubt it. He has left God out of his life and is in the process of losing the respect of his children. He may die a rich man, but he is likely to die a thousand deaths before then—deaths that involve aspects of his relationships with his wife and children, his health, his joy, his peace, his sense of fulfillment in life, and his friendships.

What the Bible Says About Money

Are you aware that more verses of Scripture are devoted to finances and money, and our proper use of them, than there are verses about heaven? God knew that money was a practical matter that would require our attention on a daily basis. Money is a vital part of our lives. We work and we expect to be paid for our work. We have bills to pay, things we need to buy with money in order to survive. We do not live in a barter society—we live in a cash-and-carry or credit-card-and-carry society.

For the most part, the Bible regards money as a medium of exchange. It is intended to be used for good and righteous purposes. It is a blessing of God given to us so that we might be stewards of a portion of the Lord's bountiful supply. In many cases, it is a tool that God uses to test our trust and faithfulness.

From cover to cover, the Bible advocates that we work diligently and honestly, and that we be generous and righteous in our handling of money. The apostle Paul taught,

> We urge you, brethren, that you increase more and more; that you also aspire to lead a quiet life, to mind your own business, and to work with your own hands, as we commanded you, that you may walk properly toward those who are outside, and that you may lack nothing. (1 Thess. 4:10–12)

The Lord expects us to work in order *not* to be in financial or material need. The Lord desires that we "increase more and more," but that we do so in a whole-person manner—spirit, mind, body, finances, and relationships all in a healthy balance.

Paul wrote to Timothy a similar message: "If anyone does not provide for his own, and especially for those of his household, he has denied the faith and is worse than an unbeliever" (1 Tim. 5:8). God expects us to work, pay our bills, and take financial responsibility for ourselves and our families. This does not mean that we need to give our children everything they desire or everything we didn't have as children. It means that we need to satisfy the basic needs of our family members: food, shelter, clothing, adequate transportation, and medical needs.

The attainment of God-given goals nearly always involves the expenditure of money or the use of material resources that God has entrusted to us. Very few goals that the Lord leads us to set for our lives can be accomplished without money. God expects us to have money and to use money, but He also expects us to have the right attitude toward money and to use money wisely in accordance with the principles of His Word.

There are two overriding principles in God's Word regarding money and material wealth:

First, God is the Source of all blessings. All wealth comes from God. Anytime you look at what you have in terms of possessions and financial holdings, you should be quick to say, "Thank God. He is the One who has given me this."

Second, there is no lasting ownership of anything material. Even the things that you believe you have bought and paid for are not things that you will own forever. All possessions become outdated, decay, or are subject to being damaged, used up, or destroyed by natural elements. All possessions are subject to being lost through theft, mismanagement (perhaps even mismanagement by someone else), or carelessness. Everything you hold in your hands is on loan from God. What matters, therefore, is that you use your possessions from God for God's purposes.

What Jesus Taught About Money

Many Christians think they know what Jesus taught about money, and most conclude that Jesus favored poverty and had very little good to say about wealth. Let's take a closer look at what Jesus and His apostles really taught about money.

First, Jesus taught that the pursuit of wealth must never be our number-one priority. Jesus gave us very solemn warnings about a love for money and the pursuit of money. He asked these questions: "For what profit is it to a man if he gains the whole world, and loses his own soul? Or what will a man give in exchange for his soul?" (Matt. 16:26).

Did Jesus teach that it was a sin for a person to be wealthy? No. Did Jesus say that all wealthy people are ungodly? No.

Rather, Jesus taught that we should not pursue money as our first priority. It should never become a substitute for seeking the kingdom of God and righteousness.

Jesus also taught that those who make wealth their number-one pursuit in life will find it very difficult to gain rewards in heaven. He said to His disciples, "Assuredly, I say to you that it is hard for a rich man to enter the kingdom of heaven. And again I say to you, it is easier for a camel to go through the eye of a needle than for a rich man to enter the kingdom of God" (Matt. 19:23–24).

In the walled cities of Jesus' time, the main gates were generally closed at nightfall. The gates were wide and tall, easily accommodating carts and camel caravans and a steady flow of two-way traffic. Built as part of the main gate of the city was a small gate just a little larger than the size of a doorway to a house. Through this small gate, a person might gain entrance to the city after dark. This smaller gate could easily be monitored and guarded. Because it was a gate within a gate, it was often called the "eye of the needle."

Could a camel get through such a small gate? Only with difficulty. To get a camel through an eye-of-the-needle gate, its driver had to completely strip it of any goods that it was carrying. Then the camel had to get down on its knees and scoot, bit by bit, almost as if crawling, through the gate. It took much effort to unload a caravan camel, much less to coax it through the small opening.

Jesus was teaching that for a rich man to gain heavenly reward, he would need to make a major effort at unburdening himself of a preoccupation with wealth and to humble himself to trust God for his security rather than trust in his money.

Never base your security on how much money you have in the bank or in mutual funds. Place your security only in the Lord. He is the One who *never* leaves you or forsakes you, and He is utterly reliable in any crisis.

Jesus was never really concerned with how much money a person might have or not have. Rather, He was intensely concerned with the attitude toward money.

Second, Jesus taught that we err greatly when we hoard our wealth and fail to give generously.

One day a man came to Jesus and said, "Teacher, tell my brother to divide the inheritance with me." Jesus replied, "Man, who made Me a judge or an arbitrator over you?"

And then Jesus said to the crowd, "Take heed and beware of covetousness, for one's life does not consist in the abundance of the things he possesses." Jesus went on to give this parable to the people gathered around Him:

The ground of a certain rich man yielded plentifully. And he thought within himself, saying, "What shall I do, since I have no room to store my crops?" So he said, "I will do this: I will pull down my barns and build greater, and there I will store all my crops and my goods. And I will say to my soul, 'Soul, you have many goods laid up for many years; take your ease; eat, drink, and be merry.'" But God said to him, "Fool! This night your soul will be required of you; then whose will those things be which you have provided?" So is he who lays up treasure for himself, and is not rich toward God. (Luke 12:16–21)

Notice that the man said, "I have no room to store *my* crops." He saw all that he had in terms of *his* crops and *his* goods and *his* bigger barn and *his* ease. He did not acknowledge God, who had allowed him to prosper.

Jesus called the man in His parable a fool not because he was wealthy, but because he had the wrong attitude about money. He was hoarding his riches and was not generous toward the things of the Lord.

In this same vein of teaching, Jesus said,

Do not lay up for yourselves treasures on earth, where moth and rust destroy and where thieves break in and steal; but lay up for yourselves treasures in heaven, where neither moth nor rust destroys and where thieves do not break in and steal. For where your treasure is, there your heart will be also. (Matt. 6:19–21)

Even if something has been in your family for years, it will not be in your family forever—unless it is something that is spiritual in nature. All things that are of a material nature ultimately belong to God and are distributed by God to human beings in order to bring about His purposes, both in individual lives and in humanity as a whole.

Only the things we do that have God's benefit, purpose, or quality associated with them are things that will last. They are the only things that will be related to our reward in heaven.

Third, Jesus taught that those who give generously to the Lord will receive generously. Jesus said, "Give, and it will be given to you: good measure, pressed down, shaken together, and running over will be put into your bosom. For with the same measure that you use, it will be measured back to you" (Luke 6:38).

What is the "it" that will be given to us as we give? It may be love, time, material provision, friendship, ideas, opportunity. When we give—and not only money, but time, energy, effort, creativity, prayer—we receive. God gives us in return precisely what we need the most, and He gives it in over-flowing supply. God desires for us to give, so that He might use what we give, multiply it, and return to us those things that will make us whole.

J. L. Kraft, the founder of Kraft Foods, knew the reality of this give-and-receive truth of God's Word. He once said, "The only investments I ever made which have paid constantly increasing dividends are those I have given to the Lord's work."

God always gives back to us in overflowing fashion. One of my pet peeves is opening a box of cereal and finding that the contents of the box are one-third air and two-thirds cereal. I am looking forward to the day when a cereal company cuts down the size of its box to match the ounces it says the box contains so that I can buy a box of my favorite cereal that is jam-packed and laced up on the outside because it's overflowing with cereal.

The Lord says plainly that if we want an overflowing blessing, we have to give in an overflowing manner. If we give with a teaspoon measure, we are going to receive a teaspoon-size supply. If we give with a giant shovel measure, we are going to receive in giant shovel amounts!

An age-old proverb states simply, "If you keep doing what you're doing, you'll keep getting what you're getting." That is especially true when it comes to money matters. If you don't like what you are getting—if you don't like the return on your investments, you don't like the results of your spending, you don't like the poverty in which you find yourself, you don't like the emptiness you feel in spite of your riches—*change what you're doing!* Appraise what you are doing with your money and how you are spending your time.

In teaching a generous return to those who give generously, Jesus was echoing the words of the prophet Malachi, who made very clear the expectation of God when it comes to giving. Malachi declared,

"Will a man rob God?
Yet you have robbed Me!
But you say,
'In what way have we robbed You?'
In tithes and offerings.
You are cursed with a curse,
For you have robbed Me,
Even this whole nation.
Bring all the tithes into the storehouse,
That there may be food in My house,
And try Me now in this,"
Says the LORD of hosts,
"If I will not open for you the windows of heaven
And pour out for you such blessing
That there will not be room enough to receive it.
And I will rebuke the devourer for your sakes,
So that he will not destroy the fruit of your ground,
Nor shall the vine fail to bear fruit for you in the field,"
Says the LORD of hosts;
"And all nations will call you blessed,

For you will be a delightful land,"
Says the LORD of hosts. (Mal. 3:8–12)

Are you robbing God today? Are you in disobedience about your giving to the Lord? Could that be the reason you are struggling in your finances? Could that be the reason your life is marked by meagerness, stinginess, and constant financial troubles and failed investments and projects?

The Lord says that those who are faithful in their giving to the Lord's work will receive an abundant blessing of ideas, opportunities, energy, health, spiritual insight, wisdom, joy, enthusiasm, goals, and yes, true godly success.

Those who fail to obey God in their giving find that their vines fail to bear fruit and the devourers steal their harvest.

You can reverse the trend through your obedience to the Lord's commandments. God rewards you, or withholds rewards from you, according to your obedience and according to the ways in which you handle money and regard money.

Money can be a dangerous thing in the hands of those who are not committed to Jesus Christ and who are not obeying God's commandments. Money can be a blessed thing in the hands of those who love the Lord and seek to obey Him in all things.

Fourth, Jesus taught that we are to be faithful stewards of all that we have, regardless of how much or little we have. Jesus taught,

He who is faithful in what is least is faithful also in much; and he who is unjust in what is least is unjust also in much. Therefore if you have not been faithful in the unrighteous mammon, who will commit to your trust the true riches? And if you have not been faithful in what is another man's, who will give you what is your own? (Luke 16:10–12)

When people hear a sermon about tithing or giving, too often they respond, "Well, I'll tithe when I make more money." The sad fact is that they won't. The person who is faithful in tithing on one dollar, two dollars, five dollars, and a hundred dollars will be faithful in tithing when he earns much more.

John D. Rockefeller once said, "I never would have been able to tithe on my first million dollars if I had not learned to tithe on my first paycheck, which was $1.50 for the week." John D. Rockefeller had a godly attitude toward money. He was perhaps the most generous philanthropist the United States has ever seen. And he also became one of the wealthiest men ever to live in America.

Material wealth is not limited to money or stocks and bonds. The house or apartment where you live is a form of material wealth. The car you drive and the things you own are forms of material wealth. When you take good care of the things the Lord has already given to you, the Lord can then entrust you with His greater riches, which include inner riches such as spiritual leadership, stewardship of the Lord's money and the property associated with the church, and the teaching of young believers in Christ Jesus. If you don't show respect for the property of your landlord or the items you have borrowed, how can you be trusted to show respect for people whom the Lord sends to you for encouragement, ministry, teaching, or wise counsel?

Most of us have lived, or will live, in an apartment or a rented house at least once in our lives. And most people who live in apartments or rental homes aspire to own their own homes. The way you treat the property you rent is going to be directly related to the way you will eventually treat your own home. God expects you to be a faithful steward of all that He has provided for you, even if it is property owned by another person.

The way you treat your company car, your office at work, and the machinery you operate in the course of doing your job should be the same way you would treat items you owned personally.

Do you really want God's overflowing blessing on your life? Then be a faithful steward of all that He gives you to use.

Fifth, Jesus taught that our stewardship is directly related to what we worship or what we serve. Jesus taught, "No servant can serve two masters; for either he will hate the one and love the other, or else he will be loyal to the one and despise the other. You cannot serve God and mammon" (Luke 16:13). The thing that is at the center of your thinking or the center of your desire is the thing you worship—it is the thing you serve, the thing you admire and respect the most, the thing for which you long the most. People whose top priority is financial gain have given money the place that belongs to God. They are guilty of idolatry.

The greedy person—the person who is never satisfied with the financial blessing he has been given—desires the blessing of money more than he desires the Giver of all blessings. He cannot be satisfied and is never truly thankful for what the Lord has given. Rather than praise God for what God has provided, the greedy person is continually looking at what he doesn't have and what he still desires to have. Greed is not related to wealth; poor people can be just as greedy as rich people.

A man spoke to me after a sermon I preached about spiritual versus material wealth, and he laughingly said, "Dr. Stanley, I don't have enough money to have a greedy attitude about it!"

The fact is, some people who have very little money are preoccupied with money. A person can be extremely poor and yet be greedy, selfish, and self-centered, and have a spirit of striving to gain money. At the opposite end of the spectrum, a person can have a great deal of money and be greedy, self-centered, and selfish, and have a spirit of striving for greater gain.

Equally true, some people are givers in their hearts and have a godly attitude toward money. Some of these people are poor, and some are rich.

One of the best ways to evaluate whom or what you are serving—God or mammon—is to analyze the expenditures in your checkbook. Your checkbook is a living testament of your faith, your obedience, and your trust in God. Where and how much you give or spend reflect your priorities. If spiritual matters are a priority in your life, spiritual matters will be a priority in your giving.

Ask yourself, In which area of my life am I growing the most?

If the answer is any area other than your spiritual life, you need to take a long, hard look at your priorities and the goals you believe God has given you.

If your primary interest is in today's interest rate rather than in what the Holy Spirit is speaking to your heart, you need to reevaluate your interests!

If your stock portfolio or your mutual fund is growing faster than your understanding of God's Word and your outreach to others in the name of Jesus Christ, your life is not in the balance that God desires.

Always, put your focus on growing in the Lord. Money may be a blessing that the Lord bestows upon you. But it must never be your goal in life or your heart's deepest desire.

Five Precautions About Money

Five major precautions in God's Word relate to the use of money and the attitude toward money.

1. Check Your Preoccupation

You must guard your mind diligently against a preoccupation with the getting and spending of money. Jesus said, "Beware of covetousness" (Luke 12:15). That verse has also been translated, "Be on your guard against every form of greed" (NASB).

A preoccupation with money can be manifested in numerous ways. It can be a constant concern with what the stock market did in the last hour, or it can be a concern with shopping all of the latest sales in the stores at the mall. Check your conversation. What do you talk about the most? Is it money or financial concerns? Check your thought life. Is money or the acquisition of material goods one of the last things you think about at night before falling asleep and one of the first things you think about when you awaken?

2. Check Your Attitude

You must guard your heart against loving money. Paul wrote to Timothy, "The love of money is a root of all kinds of evil, for which some have strayed from the faith in their greediness, and pierced themselves through with many sorrows" (1 Tim. 6:10). Paul wasn't opposed to money or its proper use. He was opposed to the love of money—a lust for material possessions to the point of greediness.

Paul advised Timothy to flee from such a love for money. He warned, "Those who desire to be rich fall into temptation and a snare, and into many foolish and harmful lusts which drown men in destruction and perdition" (1 Tim. 6:9). Paul advocated that Timothy pursue righteousness, godliness, faith, love, patience, and gentleness rather than riches. That's wise counsel for you as well.

3. Check Your Spending

You must watch what you do with your money. Money can be used for a great deal of good. But it also can be used to fund "harmful lusts," as Paul described them. Money can fund all kinds of harmful addictions.

What do you purchase with your money?

Do you gamble away the money that God causes to come into your hand?

Are you careless or frivolous in your spending habits?

Do you purchase things of poor quality or things that are a passing fad?

Do you overspend, putting yourself and your family into the bondage of debt?

Do you invest in companies that produce products that are contrary to the principles of God's Word?

Do you purchase products that promote or destroy health?

Are you generous in your giving to others?

Do you tithe?

Are you generous in supporting God's work, above your tithe?

What you do with your money is always in direct correlation to the devil's temptations or God's commands. Either you are serving God with your money, or you are yielding to the devil's temptations in the things that you purchase.

The question is sometimes asked of me, "How can I tell when I am at the limit of the amount of money and material possessions I should have?" My answer is twofold:

First, when you get to the place in your life that your concern about your money is greater than your concern with God, your relationship with God begins to cool off, and your concern with spending and enjoying material possessions heats up, you need to reevaluate your life and get your priorities back in line.

Not too long ago, a woman told me that she had been delivered from coupon clipping. I had no idea what she was talking about. She explained that she had been spending up to eight hours a week reading newspapers and magazines and clipping coupons, just so that she could save about a hundred dollars a month on her groceries and other items. She said, "I realized I was spending thirty-five hours a month clipping coupons to save a hundred dollars. It suddenly dawned on me that I would be money ahead if I worked five hours a month overtime!"

The greater admission that she made, however, was this: "I was spending far more time clipping coupons than in prayer or in the Word of God. Things are back in balance now. I work an hour a week overtime and spend at least an hour a day reading God's Word and talking things over with Him."

Second, when your possessions become a burden to you or a hindrance to your becoming involved in ministry opportunities that the Lord places before you, you need to reevaluate your material possessions.

I heard about a man who used mowing his lawn as an excuse for not getting involved in a ministry project that took place on Saturdays. I asked, "Well, how long does it take for him to mow his lawn?" The person who was telling me this story said, "He has six acres of lawn to mow, and even with a riding mulching mower, the job takes him five hours." Five hours a week mowing a lawn? Mowing instead of ministering? This man needs to readjust his priorities.

How much money can the Lord trust you with? I firmly believe that the Lord allows us to prosper financially to the degree that He can trust us to use our wealth wisely and for godly purposes.

4. Always Give Thanks

You must remember always to give thanks to the Lord for His material and financial blessings. Moses gave the Israelites a stern warning regarding this issue. He foresaw the day when they would experience a great increase in their finances, and he gave them this word from the Lord:

> When you have eaten and are full, then you shall bless the LORD your God for the good land which He has given you. Beware that you do not forget the LORD your God by not keeping His commandments, His judgments, and His statutes which I command you today, lest—when you have eaten and are full, and have built beautiful houses and dwell in them; and when your herds and your flocks multiply, and your silver and your gold are multiplied, and all that you have is multiplied; when your heart is lifted up, and you forget the LORD your God who brought you out of the land of Egypt, from the house of bondage . . . then you say in your heart, "My power and the might of my hand have gained me this wealth." And you shall remember the LORD your God, for it is He who gives you power to get wealth, that He may establish His covenant which He swore to your fathers, as it is this day. (Deut. 8:10–18)

How many times have we heard the comment, "He's a self-made man," or "He's his own man"? That kind of thinking, especially when it comes to financial wealth, is the exact opposite of the principles of God. The Bible tells us clearly that the Lord gives us the power to get wealth. He is the One who gives us creative ideas, energy, opportunities, health, and strength, and who puts together the relationships associated with our work and our moneymaking.

Don't allow anything to become more interesting to you than God. Don't allow any person to take credit for your financial gain, including yourself. To God be the praise and thanksgiving!

5. Maintain Appropriate Priorities

You must guard against a tendency to make your work and the earning of money more important to you than your pursuit of a relationship with God and the study of God's Word.

One of the most famous parables of Jesus is related to work and the use of resources. It is the teaching we know as the parable of the sower. Jesus said that a sower went out to sow, and some of the seed fell by the wayside and the birds devoured it. Some seed fell on stony ground, and it sprang up but died quickly because it had no depth to its roots. Some of the seed fell among thorns and was choked out by the thorns and produced no crop. Other seed fell on good ground and yielded a bountiful harvest.

In explaining His parable to His disciples, Jesus said this of the seed that fell among thorns:

> Now these are the ones sown among thorns; they are the ones who hear the word, and the cares of this world, the deceitfulness of riches, and the desires for other things entering in choke the word, and it becomes unfruitful. (Mark 4:18–19)

The more you earn and the more you acquire, the more you need to be in the Word of God, seeking direction and wisdom and guidance about how to *use* the money the Lord has given to you. Through my years of ministry, I have seen many people prosper in their businesses and acquire small fortunes. Unfortunately, some of these people didn't have any idea how to handle large sums of money. They didn't know how to make wise investments, how to give to ministries that were effective in spreading the gospel, or how to achieve a balance between spending and saving. Many of them lost the fortunes they had acquired.

Others who became increasingly wealthy knew how to handle their money, but they lost sight of God's purposes in giving them money. Rather than use their money to support the work of the Lord and to do good, they used their money for their selfish pleasures—for example, the purchase of a house and boat at the lake, which they felt they had to visit every weekend and which, in turn, kept them from attending church. They felt there were certain things they just had to have—many things linked to their desire for social prestige and status among their new, wealthier friends. In the end, these people may not have lost their fortunes, but they lost sight of what truly mattered in life. They lost their peace of mind, their joy in the Lord, and their inner sense of fulfillment and satisfaction.

Whether you have a little or a lot, stay in the Word of God! Listen with wide-open spiritual ears to what the Lord says to you about the proper management of the material blessings He sends your way. Be obedient in your tithing and generous in your offerings. Seek out godly counselors who are knowledgeable in how to invest money wisely. Be on guard that the devil would like nothing more than to have you use your money for *his* purposes rather than God's purposes.

8

ROADBLOCKS TO YOUR SUCCESS

Why do some people fail to reach their God-given goals and others always seem to be able to succeed in life?

A wide variety of excuses and justifications are often suggested. There are those who believe that they don't succeed because they have had a difficult family background. Others say that they had no real training, help, or encouragement to be successful. Still others cite a lack of formal education. A few point to a physical or mental disability.

These reasons are not root reasons why people fail to fulfill the goals that God has set for their lives. The root reasons that people fail to succeed lie *inside* them.

Laying Aside Every Weight

God has a plan and a will for every person. He lays before each of us a direction, a set of goals, a purpose for living. No person needs to flounder through life wondering, *Why am I here? Where am I headed?* God's Word makes it very clear why we are here and where we are going!

We are here to know Jesus Christ as our Savior and to serve Him as our Lord, wherever He leads us. We are destined for conformity to the character of Christ and to an eternal home with our heavenly Father. All other purposes for living fall under this broad, general purpose that God has for all of His children.

Why then do we flounder at times and fail to succeed in the specific individual purpose to which God has called us? Hebrews 12:1–2 offers insight into the reason:

> Therefore we also, since we are surrounded by so great a cloud of witnesses, let us lay aside every weight, and the sin which so easily ensnares us, and let us run with endurance the race that is set before us, looking unto Jesus, the author and finisher of our faith, who for the joy that was set before Him endured the cross, despising the shame, and has sat down at the right hand of the throne of God.

The good news in this passage is that you are surrounded by a host of encouragers, both those who are living and those who have gone on to be with the Lord. Countless saints of God have lived successful lives in Christ Jesus. They can, and should, inspire you. There are those alive today who are trusting in God and who are following His will for their lives. You are wise to be encouraged by them—and to seek to be like them.

I urge you to read biographies of great Christian men and women, both those in history and those who are alive today. Read about their lives and see how God has transformed them, conformed them to Christ, and worked through them to accomplish His purposes. Encourage yourself by studying their lives, always with the perspective, What God has done for others, He can and *will* do for me!

The Lord Himself should be our principal encourager. He tells us in Hebrews 13:5, "I will never leave you nor forsake you." The Lord is present with us always to help us, teach us, guide us, comfort us, and empower us. He is the One who continually speaks deep within our hearts, "You are My beloved child. I will help you succeed."

Choose to hear what the Lord speaks to you. Choose to be encouraged by His presence in your life.

The sobering news about this passage in Hebrews is that you can easily be weighed down in pursuit of God-given goals.

Have you ever tried to run a race with a fifty-pound pack strapped to your back? Have you ever tried to run with your ankles tied together? This is the picture that the writer to the Hebrews paints in describing the hindrances that can keep you from running a race successfully.

Two specific things are cited as being detrimental to your pursuit of success: *weights*—things that trouble you, weigh heavily on your mind, cause you to be worried and frustrated and discouraged; and *sins*—things that entangle you and cause you to miss out on God's blessings and opportunities. You must put down both things. Nobody else can strip these things from your life. *You* must take charge and lay aside the things that hold you back from the pursuit of godly goals. You must choose to run with endurance the race the Lord sets before you.

The Bible describes seven specific success roadblocks. All of us must deal with them, no matter what our circumstances or positions in life may be. The homemaker, president of a corporation, plumber, lawyer, doctor, janitor, preacher, salesman, carpenter, and teacher need to deal with them. God will help us deal with them, but God will not remove them from our lives apart from an active choice of the will to act against these things that hold us back and press us down.

1. The Roadblock of Fear

The first and perhaps most pervasive success roadblock is fear. Fear is the uneasy feeling that we are inadequate. It is an alarm that goes off when we feel threatened or suddenly feel incapable.

As I noted earlier in this book, fear is a major factor that keeps people from setting goals in the first place. Fear causes people to fail at what they could otherwise succeed at doing. Fear keeps people from the attainment of their goals.

I'm not talking about normal, natural fears—such as the fear of falling or the fear a child should have about walking out into busy traffic on a major highway. I'm talking about a gripping, paralyzing fear that truly is a spirit of fear. Paul wrote to Timothy, "God has not given us a spirit of fear, but of power and of love and of a sound mind" (2 Tim. 1:7).

Let me give you an example of this type of fear at work. A person is given a new position within a company or embarks upon a new vocational challenge. He believes strongly that this is what the Lord desires for him to undertake. He is excited about the challenge and believes that this new endeavor is a God-given goal for his life. He begins his new tasks with confidence and enthusiasm.

And then he realizes that he doesn't know everything there is to know to succeed in this new job or role. A huge mountain of unknowns rises up before him, which some might call a learning curve. He has more questions than answers. And the entire project or vocation suddenly seems insurmountable and overwhelming.

The more he struggles with not knowing what to do at every turn, the more he feels the criticism of others. He takes every comment to heart and agonizes over it. He feels as if he is a complete failure and he will never succeed at this new position.

Fear settles in. He becomes defensive and looks for excuses about why he is failing. He doubts his abilities and second-guesses every decision. Again and again he says, "I don't have what it takes. I can't do this. I'm scared of taking any more risks. I don't know which way to turn." And the longer that trend in thinking goes unchecked, the more he moves into sheer panic until the day comes when he wants to flee completely.

In fleeing, he does one of two things. First, he may sit down in a form of paralysis and refuse to move, isolating himself from others and withdrawing emotionally. In that state, he can quickly become discouraged and depressed. Second, he may attempt to flee by quitting the new job and perhaps even moving from the city. Either way, fear wins out, and he does not accomplish God's goal for his life.

When fear strikes you, face the fear head-on. Ask yourself, What am I really afraid of? Break down the nature of your fear. Are you afraid of failure that will lead to criticism? Are you afraid of failure that will lead to rejection from someone you love or admire? Are you afraid that your weaknesses and inadequacies will be exposed? Are you afraid that others will withdraw from you or perhaps even punish you?

Admit the fears to yourself and to God. And at times, you may be wise to admit the fears to others. In confronting and admitting your fears, you are taking a major step in overcoming them.

Then turn immediately to the matter of your faith. Faith is the opposite of fear. It is the solution for fear. Do things that build up your faith.

The first and best move you can make to build up your faith is to get your eyes off your problem and off yourself and onto Jesus. He is the Source of all your supply. He is utterly reliable and possesses all knowledge and all authority. Speak aloud the words of Hebrews 13:6 until they sink deep within your spirit:

> The LORD is my helper;
> I will not fear.
> What can man do to me?

People may criticize, reject, ridicule, and persecute, but they can't take away your salvation, your relationship with Jesus Christ, your eternal home in heaven, or the joy, contentment, and inner strength the Lord imparts to you. With Christ, you have everything that truly matters in life.

Second, ask the Lord to give you the help you need. It is one thing to say, "The Lord is my helper," and another to say, "Lord, help me today," or "Lord, help me right now in this situation." You may need an answer to a problem, friendship, a good mentor or teacher, wise counsel, or extra energy and strength. Be specific in your requests to the Lord.

Third, encourage yourself by memorizing the Word of God and quoting it as often as you need a fear-buster of inner strength. Take Isaiah 41:10–13 to heart:

> Fear not, for I am with you;
> Be not dismayed, for I am your God,
> I will strengthen you,
> Yes, I will help you,
> I will uphold you with My righteous right hand.
> Behold, all those who were incensed against you
> Shall be ashamed and disgraced;
> They shall be as nothing,
> And those who strive with you shall perish.
> You shall seek them and not find them—
> Those who contended with you.
> Those who war against you
> Shall be as nothing,
> As a nonexistent thing.
> For I, the LORD your God, will hold your right hand,
> Saying to you, "Fear not, I will help you."

Four promises are embedded in this passage:

1. The Lord promises to give us *His* presence.

2. The Lord promises to give us *His* power, which is vastly superior to our strength.

3. The Lord promises to give us *His* provision, which is more than sufficient.

4. The Lord promises to give us *His* protection against all of our enemies.

Presence, power, provision, and protection—what more could you possibly need? Remind the Lord often of His fourfold promise to you.

And, finally, ask others to pray for you. Ask them to uphold you daily in prayer, and in turn, pray for them and for their success. We read in James 5:16, "Pray for one another, that you may be healed."

What might the man in the example have done as he took his new job? First, he might have said in the face of his tremendous challenge, "I don't know all there is to know yet about this job, but the Lord knows. He will teach me, and He will help me get the information I need. He will give me discernment, wisdom, understanding, and energy to study this field and tackle this problem until I do know the information I need to know and I do have the answers I need to have."

Rather than see the job ahead as overwhelming and monumental, he might have seen it as a great mountain to be climbed, step-by-step, bit by bit. He might have said to himself at the end of each day, "The Lord helped me through another day. I learned some new things. I did good work. I took a step in the right direction."

At times of failure or error, he might have confessed errors to the Lord, asking, "Lord, help me to learn from this. Help me not to make this mistake again. Help me to remedy this error as quickly and completely as possible so that my mistake will cause no injury to the company or to any other person."

The fact is, we all fail. If you haven't failed yet at anything, trust me, you will! Every successful person has failed countless times. We all have failed to keep our word to God, to live up to what we know is right in God's eyes, and to do our best in every situation and at every task. We all have failed to be as understanding, kind, and generous as we would like to be. If we focus on our failures, we can become buried by them. The good news is that God forgives our sins and He imparts to us His Holy Spirit to help us make changes in our lives, to grow, mature, and develop so that we overcome our failures and make fewer mistakes.

Every person alive has suffered loss. We may lose something precious. But the good news is that if we obey God and continue to move forward in pursuit of the goals He has helped us to set for our lives, He is going to find a way to work all of our losses into a pattern that is positive and of eternal benefit to us. He will make us strong in areas where we have been weak. He will give us victories and rewards in areas where we have suffered loss in the past. He will turn *all* things to good. (See Rom. 8:28.)

It is also a fact that you will never please everybody. There will always be somebody who will criticize what you do, even if you have the most impeccable character and integrity of any man or woman on the face of the earth. Seek to please the Lord. Seek to fulfill what He has called you to do. And let the criticism of others flow by you. Don't internalize their negative comments. Don't take them to heart or allow them to dictate what you do.

This is not to say that you should reject all godly counsel. Rather, you should reject all criticism aimed at destroying you, diminishing you, or discouraging you. The Lord never comes to steal, kill, or destroy you. That is the work of the enemy. (See John 10:10.)

Don't be surprised when fear emerges. Nothing good in life comes without a struggle against fear. The key is to run headlong at fear with your faith in Christ Jesus and your confidence firmly set in Him. You can overcome fear, and it is up to you to break through this success roadblock each and every time it rears its ugly head.

2. The Roadblock of Doubt

A success roadblock closely related to fear is doubt. Doubt is a lack of assurance. When we doubt, we become unsteady, tentative, and wavering in our pursuit of a goal. We may not become paralyzed or be put into "flight" mode as with fear, but we may become bogged down and miss important opportunities for advancement.

Believing you can achieve a God-given goal is vital to *reaching* a God-given goal. The writer of Hebrews stated, "Without faith it is impossible to please Him, for he who comes to God must believe that He is, and that He is a rewarder of those who diligently seek Him" (11:6). How do you please God? You please Him by receiving His Son, Jesus Christ, as your Savior, and by obeying Him day by day. Part of your obeying God is doing what God tells you to do, not only in the commandments of the Bible, but in the pursuit of goals that God has designed for you. Without faith in God—and without believing that God desires to reward you and will reward you as you diligently seek to follow Him—you fail.

As with fears, you must face doubts head-on. You must ask, Why am I doubting? There are several reasons for doubt. One is a lack of understanding that God is with you always. Anytime you are concerned about whether God is with you, I encourage you to read aloud one of these passages of the Bible as often as you need to read it until you truly believe it:

- Philippians 4:13: "I can do all things through Christ who strengthens me."

- Philippians 4:19: "My God shall supply all your need according to His riches in glory by Christ Jesus."

- Hebrews 13:5: "I will never leave you nor forsake you."

- John 16:24: "Until now you have asked nothing in My name. Ask, and you will receive, that your joy may be full."

- Matthew 7:7: "Ask, and it will be given to you; seek, and you will find; knock, and it will be opened to you."

When I experience momentary doubt, I usually get on my knees, open my Bible, and read it aloud to God, saying, "Lord, this is what You have said in Your Word. I trust You to do this in *my* life."

Doubt Caused by Past Failures. Another reason that people doubt is their past failures. They conclude that because they failed once in the past—or perhaps even several times—God isn't with them and they are bound to fail again.

Most of us need to stop looking over our shoulders at our past mistakes. To do so is to continue to carry guilt with us over sins that the Lord has already forgiven and forgotten. When we continue to bemoan past failures—even though we have confessed those sins and failures to God, been forgiven for them, and made a decision with our wills to repent of them and change our ways—we are stating that we have not been able to forgive ourselves. We are carrying excess and unnecessary baggage in our lives.

If God has forgiven you, which He says He does *every time you confess your sins to Him,* then forgive yourself! (See 1 John 1:9.)

The more you cling to past failures and cause them to produce doubt in your life, the more you destroy your confidence in the Lord. You begin to see yourself as a failure that God cannot use, a "mistake" that God has made, an unworthy person whom God cannot redeem or use for His purposes. That thinking is unscriptural. You have never made a mistake that God cannot forgive, remedy, and work toward your good eventually. You don't have the ability to mess up so much that God will reject you or turn away from using you. You cannot undo the bonds of love that He has wrapped all around you.

If you think you are a failure, you'll act like a failure, and the things you attempt to do will fail. Choose to lay down your failure mentality, and see yourself as a beloved, talented, and spiritually gifted child of God. Act as the saved, Holy Spirit–filled, on-your-way-to-being-conformed-to-Christ person that you are!

Don't wait for others to do what you must do. Yet another reason that people doubt is that they expect others to provide opportunities and blessings to help them succeed. They wait for someone else to do the believing and to do the work necessary to accomplish a goal. When that someone else doesn't show up, they begin to doubt.

God expects you to reach the goals that He has designed uniquely and individually for you. Nobody else can do what He created you to do. Nobody else can do the believing and the work necessary to accomplish the goals He has set before you.

Take God at His Word! Many people doubt because they do not take God at His word. They read the Bible but then conclude, "That's for somebody else." What you read in the Scriptures is for *you.* Count on it.

James wrote about this:

If any of you lacks wisdom [and we could insert here *anything* that we need or lack], let him ask of God, who gives to all liberally and without reproach, and it will be given to him. But let him ask in faith, with no doubting, for he who doubts is like a wave of the sea driven and tossed by the wind. For let not that man suppose that he will receive anything from the Lord; he is a double-minded man, unstable in all his ways. (James 1:5–8)

The person who is wishy-washy in his pursuit of a goal, emotionally unsteady and uncertain about what he believes to be God's truth and God's promises, sets himself up for failure. Nobody else can be blamed.

On the other hand, Jesus gave us great encouragement about what happens to those who face situations with faith rather than doubt. He taught:

Have faith in God. For assuredly, I say to you, whoever says to this mountain, "Be removed and be cast into the sea," and does not doubt in his heart, but believes that those things he says will be done, he will have whatever he says. Therefore I say to you, whatever things you ask when you pray, believe that you receive them, and you will have them. (Mark 11:22–24)

You must not be unrealistic in pursuit of a God-given goal. The removal of a mountain may take time—in some cases, years or decades. But if you are steady in your pursuit of the goal, the mountain will go, the obstacles will be overcome, the roadblocks will be removed. You must not set yourself up for doubt by thinking that you can accomplish everything in a day.

Consider for a moment a young man who may be called to preach the gospel. If the Lord said, "I expect you to produce fifty years' worth of sermons in your lifetime," that young man would probably collapse immediately. Rather, the Lord in His mercy says, "I set before you the goal of preaching the gospel as long as you are alive, as effectively and irresistibly and powerfully and plainly as you can." That's a goal a person can begin to pursue. And if he lives long enough, he'll have sermons for fifty years.

The end goal of a lifetime of preaching, however, is not where this young preacher needs to set his eyes. He needs to say, "What is the best possible sermon I can preach next Sunday? What does the Lord want to say through me to the people in my church *this week?*" The preacher is likely to have the faith to believe God for a good sermon this week and next week and the next week and the next week, one at a time.

You need to focus your faith on your immediate and short-range goals. Your faith will be most effective and potent there. And over time, your faith will be strengthened so that your immediate and short-range goals become more challenging. Only as you look back will you be able to say, "I lived by faith." And that, of course, is precisely the way the Lord calls you to live:

The just shall live by faith. (Heb. 10:38)

We walk by faith, not by sight. (2 Cor. 5:7)

The life which I now live in the flesh I live by faith in the Son of God, who loved me and gave Himself for me. (Gal. 2:20)

3. The Roadblock of Excuse-itis

Excuse-itis is a disease of the soul. It is an infection of excuses and self-justifications that takes root and affects the whole of a person's desire to pursue a God-given goal to its completion. Countless people are infected with this spiritual sickness.

Excuse-itis is the habit of excusing ourselves or offering an excuse at every turn for *not* doing what we know to do. It is the cornerstone of the blame game—blaming the way we feel physically, blaming the poor parenting we had, blaming the fact that we were mistreated at some time in our lives, blaming our failure on the fact that we don't have a car or don't have enough money or don't have this or that.

Excuse-itis is as old as man—in fact, as old as the first man and woman. Adam blamed Eve for his eating the apple. Eve blamed the devil for enticing her. And excuse-itis got them nowhere with God. Excuses didn't count for them, and they don't count for us.

When the Lord first called Moses to return to Egypt and say to Pharaoh, "Let My people go," Moses sputtered excuses. He said, "I'm a nobody," "I'm a lousy public speaker," "I'm not credible with the people," "I'm a has-been." God didn't accept any of Moses' excuses, and He won't accept ours.

How many excuses does God accept for our disobeying Him or failing to pursue the goals He has put before us? Not one.

"But what," you may say, "about my situation? I would love to teach

Sunday school, but the Lord knows I'm not trained as a teacher. I can't teach without training." My answer would be, "Get trained!"

"But what," you may say, "can I do? My schedule is already overbooked. I don't have time to take on this new challenge." My answer: "Change your schedule."

"But," you may say, "I just can't work with these people around me and still pursue my God-given goals." My answer: "Associate with a new group of people, but first check your attitude and behavior. Those people may not be the problem. You may be the problem."

Jesus told a parable about a rich man who went on a journey and entrusted his wealth to three servants. To one, he gave five talents; to another, two talents; and to a third, just one talent. When the master returned, he found that the first two servants had doubled his money in his absence. The third servant, however, got into excuse-itis. He said, "Lord, I knew you to be a hard man, reaping where you have not sown, and gathering where you have not scattered seed. And I was afraid, and went and hid your talent in the ground. Look, there you have what is yours" (Matt. 25:24–25). How did the master respond? He called this servant "wicked and lazy," and he took the talent from him and gave it to the one who had produced ten talents.

Never try to blame another person for your failure. That includes your spouse, your boss, your parent, your child, your pastor, your best friend, your doctor, or any other person you encounter. God has given you talents and spiritual gifts He expects you to use, without excuse.

There are no good excuses for failing to go to church, read the Bible, pray, share your faith, use your mind, believe God, work to the best of your physical ability, give to God and others, or love others generously.

In my experience, I have concluded that if most people would redirect the energy they put into concocting excuses into genuine effort, they would have no cause to make excuses. They'd be succeeding!

One practical way to overcome excuse-itis is to become involved in a group. One woman told me that she had a difficult time disciplining herself to study the Bible, so she decided to start a Bible study group that met in her home. Another person told me that he got over excuse-itis by signing up for lessons and putting down an advance payment on them. That motivated him to quit making excuses and get busy pursuing a goal he believed God had helped him set.

Take a look at your life. What excuses are you giving to yourself and others for your continuing to live at a level that is less than what God desires for you? Isn't it time you got busy and got rid of those excuses?

4. The Roadblock of Procrastination

Procrastination is putting off until tomorrow what you know you should do today. Very often the surface reason for procrastination is fear, doubt, or excuses, but at the core of procrastination is a lack of motivation.

As healthy citizens living in a free nation, the vast majority of us do what we *want* to do. We find time and energy for the things we want to do. We find the money for the things we want to purchase. When we procrastinate in the pursuit of our God-given goals, we are saying, "There's something more important to me than obeying God and moving into the success level that He desires for me."

Two types of people are especially prone to procrastination. The first is the perfectionist. A perfectionist is not simply a person who does the best he can at the things he undertakes. A perfectionist feels driven to do everything perfectly. A perfectionist is often reluctant to begin certain tasks or projects, probably because he anticipates the possibility or inevitability of falling short of perfection.

In the early days of my ministry, I put off a number of tasks that I either didn't particularly enjoy doing or didn't feel adequate to do—from returning phone calls to writing out outlines for my sermons. I felt more miserable the more I put things off, and eventually I came to grips with the fact that I was not eliminating my pain. I was only delaying and prolonging it.

The perfectionist often stretches out a task much longer than necessary as he strives to make every detail perfect. Immediate goals often turn into short-range goals, which in turn tend to stretch into long-range goals. For the perfectionist, to complete a task or to reach a goal is almost a sign of failure because he is sure that something is still wrong with the job that he has done.

The second type of person prone to procrastination is the discomfort dodger. This person knows that the accomplishment of any goal takes a certain amount of effort, energy, and saying no to frivolous pleasures and fleshly lusts. The discomfort dodger would rather take his ease than expend the effort necessary for attaining a goal. Or he may seek to avoid the possible emotional discomforts of embarrassment or rejection as the result of failing or falling short of expectations. He may buy into the idea, "If I don't make an effort today, I can't be criticized for what I do today."

If you are procrastinating in the pursuit of a godly goal, ask yourself *why*. Are you in bondage to perfectionism? Are you trying to dodge discomfort?

If so, you need to ask the Lord to free you of perfectionism. Nobody is perfect except God. He doesn't expect you to be perfect. He knows all about your imperfections, yet He chooses to reside in you by the power of the Holy Spirit to help you overcome your imperfections. The perfecting work is *His,* not yours.

If you are dodging discomfort, ask the Lord to help you overcome this emotional laziness. Find ways of motivating yourself to take action. Set up rewards for yourself for accomplishing immediate and short-range goals.

One of the most positive steps for a procrastinator or a person who is prone to excuse-itis is to make himself accountable to another Christian. Ask someone you know and respect to work with you as an accountability partner. Ask this person to hold you responsible for wasting time and for putting off the positive steps you know you should take toward the godly goals you have set. At times, this person may be a good person to work with you in the pursuit of your goal—for example, if you have set a goal of walking daily, perhaps your accountability partner will walk with you. If you have a goal of reading your Bible daily, perhaps your accountability partner can join you and you can read the Bible aloud to each other, or you can phone each other and spend five minutes sharing the key insights you have gleaned from that day's reading.

Too many believers fall into a lifestyle of procrastination when it comes to making important changes in their lives, especially changes related to their spiritual disciplines and their health habits. Find someone who can motivate you to start these major changes and who will help you stay motivated over time.

If you are a procrastinator, I offer you this very practical tip: sit down before you go to bed tonight, and write down one thing that you are going to accomplish tomorrow. Choose a task related to an immediate, short-range, or long-range goal. Put down a time frame next to that item. If the activity or chore you have listed is likely to take you longer than an hour, break the larger task down into smaller pieces, and list only one piece of the larger job.

Ask the Lord to help you accomplish that one thing within the next twenty-four hours. Since you know the rest of your schedule for the coming day, you may need to set your alarm clock for a half hour earlier so you can get a head start on your goal. You may need to shorten a lunch hour. Do whatever you need to do to adjust your schedule in order to give yourself the time to do that one thing.

Follow the same procedure every night this week. And then designate a small reward for accomplishing a week's worth of immediate goals. Your self-given reward may be a fifteen-minute hot bath at the end of the day, dining out on Saturday night, or something else that is pleasurable to you.

Take time to reflect at the end of the week that you have done seven things toward reaching your goals that you probably wouldn't have done otherwise. Find joy in the steps you have taken. Thank the Lord for helping you overcome your procrastination tendencies. And then set a goal for the next day.

We learn to walk by taking one step and then two steps and then three steps. A long-distance trip by car is accomplished a mile at a time. A debt is paid off one payment at a time. Choose to take small, even steps *daily*.

5. The Roadblock of Greed

Greed is an insatiable hunger or craving for acquiring more than a person needs. Greed has no bottom to it. It can never be satisfied. The greedy person never has enough.

If you have a deep desire to be rich or to make a lot of money, you need to ask yourself *why*. Why do you want to be wealthy? Is it to be able to boast of your wealth? Is it to be able to leave a large inheritance and win the love of your family? Is it to be able to exert power and influence over other people? Is it to give yourself feelings of security? These reasons are not in keeping with God's Word. Ask the Lord why you feel the need to amass wealth. Ask the Lord what goal *He* would desire for you to have when it comes to your finances.

How does greed create a stumbling block for reaching goals? It tends to happen in this way. Greed functions in the natural world—the material, financial, practical world of the senses. The greedy person wants one more dollar, one more acquisition, one more suit, one more taste, one more fix or pill, one more of whatever he craves. And the more he pursues that one more thing, the less he has eyes for true spiritual concerns. The pursuit of the natural world supersedes all desire to pursue the things of God. When that happens, the person's life falls out of balance.

The Lord's desire is that we develop an ever-increasing longing for becoming like Christ and for doing the things that the Lord leads us to do. Most of the things that the Lord will lead us to do will build up the spirit rather than gratify the flesh. To fall into greed is to move in the exact opposite direction of what God desires.

The greedy person also tends to wall off other people. The greedy person builds an emotional and sometimes a literal fence around what he possesses and says to others, "Keep out. Don't touch. This is mine!" Such a person rarely extends himself in ministry to others and tends to be very critical of those who have not acquired as much stuff as he has acquired. In comparison, the godly person says, "Let me help you reach your goals. I know in helping you, I will be acting in a way that is pleasing to the Lord. I will trust Him to provide the help that I need to reach the goals He has set for my life."

There is no way a person can practice greed without stepping on somebody else's toes. Those who are consumed with greed misuse, abuse, and take advantage of other people. They are on an unending quest to move more and more worldly goods under their control or use more and more things for their personal pleasure. Greed is directly linked to covetousness—wanting what someone else has and is rightfully his.

The Bible strongly opposes greed. Jesus taught, "Beware, and be on your guard against every form of greed; for not even when one has an abundance does his life consist of his possessions" (Luke 12:15 NASB).

The apostle Paul wrote to the Ephesians: "Do not let immorality or any impurity or greed even be named among you, as is proper among saints" (Eph. 5:3 NASB).

Greed is an idolatrous attitude. It is desiring the things of the natural and material world more than the things of God. Paul wrote very plainly about this subject to the Colossians: "Therefore consider the members of your earthly body as dead to immorality, impurity, passion, evil desire, and greed, which amounts to idolatry" (Col. 3:5 NASB).

I have never met a happy greedy person. I have never met a contented, peaceful greedy person. The greedy person has an agitated soul, a constant feeling of unhappiness that he doesn't yet possess all that he desires.

I recommend a very practical step to help a person deal with greed: give away something that you value. Anytime I feel I am clinging too tightly to something, I make a gift of that item. Nothing is worth holding on to if it means developing a spirit of greed or disobeying God. Greed doesn't fit the character of a Christian. We must actively choose to cast it away from our lives.

A second major way to confront greed is to make a conscious effort to tithe and give offerings. Greedy people are rarely tithers. Begin tithing. Give generous offerings to God's work. Remember the words of the apostle Paul:

> Command those who are rich in this present age not to be haughty, nor to trust in uncertain riches but in the living God, who gives us richly all things to enjoy. Let them do good, that they be rich in good works, ready to give, willing to share, storing up for themselves a good foundation for the time to come, that they may lay hold on eternal life. (1 Tim. 6:17–19)

6. The Roadblock of Sin

One way of stating this success roadblock is the violation of the conscience. Your conscience acts as an internal alarm system in your spirit and soul. You may call it a bell or a red light—whatever term you use, your conscience is a signal to your inner self that you are on dangerous ground and that you have either entered into or are about to enter into a "sin zone." Your conscience warns you against the behavioral and attitudinal moral dangers that can lead to your destruction.

The person who willfully violates his conscience again and again sears himself against an awareness and an abhorrence of sin. Paul warned Timothy, "Some will depart from the faith, . . . speaking lies in hypocrisy, having their own conscience seared with a hot iron" (1 Tim. 4:1–2). The more someone willfully violates his conscience and proceeds to sin, the less regard he has for the warning signals of his conscience. Eventually, he won't experience *any* warning in the inner person regarding sin. The ability to discern evil becomes inoperative.

Such a person is on dangerous ground because he has little understanding of what is right and wrong. Therefore, he has little understanding of what God desires for him to set as good goals that will result in godly success.

Can a person attain the goals that God has set for his life if he has a seared conscience and repeatedly enters into sin? No. The pursuit of God's will for a person's life is the exact opposite of the pursuit of fleshly desires. To set godly goals and to pursue them with enthusiasm, a person must be willing to turn away from sin and reject every temptation to sin.

Correct programming is required. The problem with the conscience is that we can trust it only if it is programmed correctly. If we have programmed the conscience according to the principles of God, we can trust the conscience. But if we have programmed it according to any other set of standards or principles, we cannot trust it.

A conscience that has been programmed incorrectly is a major detriment to determining and to pursuing God's goals for one's life. God will not enable a person to succeed if he deliberately and willfully chooses to violate God's Word and pursue his self-made goals rather than God's goals.

A person without a conscience is like a car without brakes. There is no "slow down" or "stop" mechanism. The person without a conscience moves headlong into sin. And such a person reaps the full negative harvest of sin.

I realized one day that I was being very complimentary and helpful to a particular person who had mentioned that he wanted to give me a large gift of money for the ministry. I began to feel uneasy in my spirit, and I asked the Lord what was wrong. The Lord spoke very directly to me, "You're manipulating this situation. Stop it. Trust Me."

When you feel a nagging, gnawing feeling deep in your heart, don't ignore it. Go to God with it. Give Him an opportunity to speak to you His desires regarding your attitude or behavior.

7. The Roadblock of Slothfulness

Slothfulness is a big term for the four-letter word *lazy.* In the Bible, being slothful is contrasted to being industrious or working diligently. The slothful person seeks to get by with minimal effort, minimal expenditure of creativity and energy, and minimal involvement with others.

The pursuit of godly goals takes energy. The building of godly relationships takes effort. The slothful person doesn't want to extend himself to people or to the pursuit of goals.

The slothful person doesn't want the discomfort or pain that comes with hard work. He doesn't want the pain that can come from being vulnerable to others.

Overtime hours? The slothful person says, "No way."

Take on a new responsibility? "No way."

Go out of his way to bless another person? "No way."

Friend, there is no way the slothful person is going to be successful!

Three Lies the Slothful Believe. There are several lies that the slothful person nearly always buys into:

1. "You can work smarter, not harder." No goal worth achieving is ever achieved by merely being smart. Every goal requires working hard—long hours, extra effort, more study, greater intensity of preparation.

2. "Don't let others use you. Give the minimum you can give or people will take advantage of you." God intends for us to be involved with other people and to be generous toward them. Only when we give our best to others do we put ourselves in a position to receive God's best. Paul wrote this to the slaves who were part of the church in Ephesus:

> Bondservants, be obedient to those who are your masters according to the flesh, with fear and trembling, in sincerity of heart, as to Christ; not with eyeservice, as menpleasers, but as bondservants of Christ, doing the will of God from the heart, with goodwill doing service, as to the Lord, and not to men, knowing that whatever good anyone does, he will receive the same from the Lord, whether he is a slave or free. (Eph. 6:5–8)

3. "There's no point in getting all riled up. Relax. Enjoy life. Smell the roses." The Lord certainly intends for us to enjoy life. He desires for us to take time to smell the roses, but He likely intends for us to smell the roses while we're tilling the garden. The Bible has very strong words about idle people.

Read through these verses for a brief example of the Bible's teachings on this matter of laziness:

He who is slothful in his work
Is a brother to him who is a great destroyer. (Prov. 18:9)

I went by the field of the lazy man,
And by the vineyard of the man devoid of understanding;
And there it was, all overgrown with thorns;
Its surface was covered with nettles;
Its stone wall was broken down.
When I saw it, I considered it well;
I looked on it and received instruction:
A little sleep, a little slumber,
A little folding of the hands to rest;
So shall your poverty come like a prowler,
And your need like an armed man. (Prov. 24:30–34)

Because of laziness the building decays,
And through idleness of hands the house leaks. (Eccl. 10:18)

For even when we were with you, we commanded you this: If anyone will not work, neither shall he eat. For we hear that there are some who walk among you in a disorderly manner, not working at all, but are busybodies. Now those who are such we command and exhort through our Lord Jesus Christ that they work in quietness and eat their own bread. (2 Thess. 3:10–12)

My mother was a hard worker, and she required me to work from such a young age that I don't think I've ever had a problem with being slothful. If anything, I have a tendency to work too much.

If you tend to be slothful, recognize that you are being a detriment to your family, your employer, or any other group in which you are involved. Find something that motivates you to get up and get moving.

An Awesome Future Ahead

You and I have been given the awesome promise and presence of the Holy Spirit living inside us to enable us to achieve everything that God has set out for us. The Holy Spirit will help us remove these roadblocks when we ask for His help. But the Holy Spirit will not override personal will or sovereignly remove these roadblocks *unless we invite Him to help us.*

Are you in fear today regarding the goals God has given you?

Are you doubting that God is with you in the pursuit of your goals or that He will enable you to succeed in them?

Are you making excuses rather than making progress?

Are you procrastinating in doing what you know the Lord desires for you to be doing?

Are you in greed?

Are you violating your conscience regarding God's goals? Are you engaging in activities and attitudes you know to be sinful?

Are you slothful, standing by idly when you could be working on your goals?

If your answer is yes to any of these questions, confess your need to the Lord. Ask Him to forgive you. And then ask Him to help you move forward in your life. Become involved with others who can help you overcome these roadblocks in your life. Push them aside, one by one, and take the next step necessary to pursue your goals.

9

THE ATTITUDE REQUIRED FOR SUCCESS

Lisa remembers her grandmother gently teasing her about being "Melissa Melancholy." For much of Lisa's life, she has felt a little melancholy or blue. Although she has never been able to pinpoint the exact origin of her depression, and although her depression has never reached clinical proportions, Lisa admits that she has always felt a little down and that she rather enjoys feeling sad at times. Friends have teased her about not smiling, and more than one boyfriend has encouraged her to lighten up in her approach to life.

Recently Lisa noticed that several of her coworkers have been receiving promotions. She knows that her work has been on par with theirs and that she has more seniority than one coworker who was promoted. Why not me? she asked herself.

Roger had a rough childhood. His parents divorced when he was three, and then his mother abandoned him, leaving Roger in the care of his grandmother. For much of his childhood Roger lived in poverty. Since his grandmother worked full-time, he didn't receive much personal attention. And given his general emotional struggles, he found it difficult to concentrate and tended to do poorly in school.

As an adult, Roger makes no secret of the bad breaks he experienced as a child. He lets just about every person within earshot know that he deserved a better childhood and that he hasn't succeeded to any greater degree as a young adult because of the poor parenting of his parents, the lack of attention from his grandmother, and the lack of understanding and compassion of his childhood teachers. Roger is also quick to express his frustration that nobody seems willing to help him get ahead.

Georgia, by her own admission, is a green-eyed girl. She admits to liking nice things, including things that belong to others and that she wishes were hers. She is envious of her supervisor's office, her best friend's husband, and her brother's car. Her favorite phrase is, "Someday I'm going to have . . ." Much of her conversation is devoted to things she intends to buy, obtain, or manipulate her way into. She just can't understand why she hasn't already acquired more.

Lisa, Roger, and Georgia have not yet learned a key principle related to success: *Your attitude shapes your future.*

What you believe gives rise both to what you feel and how you respond to life. Your attitude produces behavior. And what you do is directly related to what you become as a person and what you succeed in accomplishing.

The Key That Gives Rise to Success

Jesus made a statement that is perhaps the most important key to success you will ever encounter. It frames an attitude that gives rise to success. It is a principle so basic that a child can understand it. And yet it is a principle so profound that none of us, acting in our own strength alone, can live it out fully. We must have the Holy Spirit's help if we are to have this attitude and act on it. Jesus taught, "Whatever you want men to do to you, do also to them" (Matt. 7:12).

Most of us have learned this golden rule from childhood: do unto others as you would have them do unto you. But I want you to see today the context for this teaching of Jesus:

> Ask, and it will be given to you; seek, and you will find; knock, and it will be opened to you. For everyone who asks receives, and he who seeks finds, and to him who knocks it will be opened. Or what man is there among you who, if his son asks for bread, will give him a stone? Or if he asks for a fish, will he give him a serpent? If you then, being evil, know how to give good gifts to your children, how much more will your Father who is in heaven give good things to those who ask Him! Therefore, whatever you want men to do to you, do also to them, for this is the Law and the Prophets. (Matt. 7:7–12)

This statement that we have come to call the golden rule of behavior is a statement that Jesus made in the context of our getting our needs met and our accomplishing the things that the Lord desires us to be and do. Jesus was challenging the people to ask the Lord for His blessings—truly to ask the Lord, "What is Your will for my life? What do You want me to do? What have You planned for my success? What will make me a success in Your eyes?"

He admonished the people to seek the things that the Lord revealed as being important and blessed. He said, "Pursue the goodness of God. Seek righteousness."

Jesus taught them to persist in their quest for God's blessings and God's success until they attained them. The tense of the verbs *ask, seek,* and *knock* in the original language in which they were written probably should have been translated "ask and keep on asking, seek and keep on seeking, knock and keep on knocking." According to Jesus, we should always be in a state of asking the Lord, "What do You want me to do today? What will be pleasing to You? What will be the right thing for me to pursue right now so that I might be and do what You desire for me to be and do?"

Jesus followed His commands to ask, seek, and knock by saying, "And the Lord will answer you. He will cause you to find what you are seeking. He will open the fullness of His riches and His presence to you. If other people give to you what you request of them, and if parents give to their children what their children need even if they don't know to request what they need, how much more the Father will give to you."

Then Jesus concluded by teaching, "If you live in right standing with other people, treating them as you treat yourself, you will be blessed by the Lord and by men."

In the gospel of Luke we find a similar teaching of Jesus: "Therefore be merciful, just as your Father also is merciful. Judge not, and you shall not be judged. Condemn not, and you shall not be condemned. Forgive, and you will be forgiven. Give, and it will be given to you" (Luke 6:36–38). The Lord evaluates us, forgives us, and rewards us in direct proportion to the way we think and act toward other people.

Too many people like to overlook and try to dismiss this principle of God's Word. Many Christians are quick to say, "The Lord judges me solely on what I do in relationship to the Lord." That simply isn't what the Bible says. The Bible teaches that the Lord judges us on the basis of what we do with regard to Him *and with regard to others.*

Our Thoughts Are About Others

You may say, "Well, the Lord looks on my heart." Indeed, He does. But what have you spent most of your time pondering in your heart? It is virtually impossible for you to think thoughts that do not involve other people. A high percentage of our thoughts, opinions, and feelings on any given day are in direct relationship to what others are doing and saying. Most of our prayers are for ourselves and other people. Most of our praise is about what God has done in our lives and in the lives of other people.

The Lord looks on the heart, but our hearts look on both God and others.

The same is true for our behavior. The Lord doesn't limit His evaluation of us on the basis of our hearts. He also evaluates our actions. And most of our actions involve other people to some degree.

The person who talks only to himself, cares only for himself, and responds only to himself is considered mentally insane. We cannot help being involved with other people and expressing our attitudes toward them through our actions if we are living normal, healthy lives.

The Lord Responds to Our Behavior Toward Others

Consider these verses that speak of how the Lord responds to us on the basis of our behavior toward others. Jesus taught:

> If you forgive men their trespasses, your heavenly Father will also forgive you. But if you do not forgive men their trespasses, neither will your Father forgive your trespasses. (Matt. 6:14)

> For with what judgment you judge, you will be judged; and with the same measure you use, it will be measured back to you. (Matt. 7:2)

> Not everyone who says to Me, "Lord, Lord," shall enter the kingdom of heaven, but he who does the will of My Father in heaven. Many will say to Me in that day, "Lord, Lord, have we not prophesied in Your name, cast out demons in Your name, and done many wonders in Your name?" And then I will declare to them, "I never knew you; depart from Me, you who practice lawlessness!" (Matt. 7:21–23)

> You did not choose Me, but I chose you and appointed you that you should go and bear fruit, and that your fruit should remain, that whatever you ask the Father in My name He may give you. These things I command you, that you love one another. (John 15:16–17)

In teaching about the way we relate to others, Jesus nearly always went beyond the letter of the law to the real spirit of the law. He spoke repeatedly of the importance of our thinking and our attitudes toward others:

You have heard that it was said to those of old, "You shall not commit adultery." But I say to you that whoever looks at a woman to lust for her has already committed adultery with her in his heart. (Matt. 5:27–28)

You have heard that it was said to those of old, "You shall not murder, and whoever murders will be in danger of the judgment." But I say to you that whoever is angry with his brother without a cause shall be in danger of the judgment. And whoever says to his brother, "Raca!" shall be in danger of the council. But whoever says, "You fool!" shall be in danger of hell fire. (Matt. 5:21–22)

You have heard that it was said, "You shall love your neighbor and hate your enemy." But I say to you, love your enemies, bless those who curse you, do good to those who hate you, and pray for those who spitefully use you and persecute you, that you may be sons of your Father in heaven. (Matt. 5:43–45)

Jesus noted that the golden rule *fulfills* the Law and the Prophets—it sums them up. The Law contains very strong commandments about how people should relate to one another morally and ethically. Six of the Ten Commandments deal directly with interpersonal relationships: children are commanded to honor their parents, and the Lord commands us not to murder, commit adultery, steal, bear false witness against our neighbors, or covet our neighbors' possessions.

In the book of Deuteronomy, Moses commanded the Israelites to keep *all* of the laws and statutes that the Lord had given to them, and he also gave a strong warning that the Lord's "curse" would be on those who disobeyed very specific commandments. In Deuteronomy 27:15–26, we find a list of behaviors that bring about the Lord's harshest judgment. As you read through this list, note that seven of these nine statements deal with behavior toward other people:

- "The one who makes a carved or molded image, an abomination to the LORD, the work of the hands of the craftsman, and sets it up in secret"
- "The one who treats his father or his mother with contempt"
- "The one who moves his neighbor's landmark"
- "The one who makes the blind to wander off the road"
- "The one who perverts the justice due the stranger, the fatherless, and widow"
- "The one who lies with his father's wife . . . any kind of animal . . . his sister . . . his mother-in-law"
- "The one who attacks his neighbor secretly"
- "The one who takes a bribe to slay an innocent person"
- "The one who does not confirm all the words of this law"

The judgment of God is not only on how we worship God, but on how we behave toward others, which includes how we think about others.

One day a temple lawyer asked Jesus, "Teacher, which is the great commandment in the law?" Jesus replied, "'You shall love the LORD your God with all your heart, with all your soul, and with all your mind.' This is the first and great commandment. And the second is like it: 'You shall love your neighbor as yourself'" (Matt. 22:36–39). Jesus placed loving our neighbors on par with our love of God.

A Commandment, Not a Suggestion

God's command that we behave toward others as we would like them to treat us is not a suggestion; it is a requirement. We have absolutely no basis for attaining godly goals or seeking God's blessings and God's rewards unless we are willing first to take a look at our attitudes and behavior toward other people. Our success depends upon the way we treat others.

How Do You Want Others to Treat You?

Two of the key questions you must ask as you pursue God's goals for your life are these: How do I want to be treated by other people? Am I willing to treat others in the same way?

You probably won't have any trouble answering the first question. Take a look at this list of opposites and you'll likely choose all of the behaviors and attitudes in the left-hand column. No one wants to be treated in the ways listed in the right-hand column:

Acceptance	Rejection
Kindness	Rudeness
Understanding	Insensitivity
Care	Indifference
Helpfulness	Opposition
Love	Hate
Support	Persecution
Encouragement	Discouragement
Generosity	Stinginess, selfishness
Forgiveness	Revenge, unforgiveness
Loyalty	Disloyalty

The more difficult question to answer is, Am I willing to treat others in the ways listed in the left-hand column? You would say yes—in theory. But then you may put qualifiers on these behaviors: "Yes, I treat people this way if . . ." or "when . . ." or "depending upon . . ." You may put qualifiers on the times when you will be loving, forgiving, loyal, generous, and so forth.

You may say to yourself, "I love being accepting and supportive and helpful to those who are my friends," or "I am always kind and caring to those who are kind and caring to me." In making such statements, you are turning around Jesus' words 180 degrees. You are saying, "I'll do to others what they do to me first." Jesus says, "You act *first* and respond in the way you want to be treated, regardless of what others do to you."

You need to face up to several facts about human behavior:

First, all of us who seek to live a godly life are going to be persecuted. You are going to be persecuted in your business, in your vocation, and among your friends. You are going to be misused and abused—verbally and emotionally and perhaps physically. We live in a fallen world and sinful man is always abusive. Paul counseled Timothy, "All who desire to live godly in Christ Jesus will suffer persecution" (2 Tim. 3:12). Not only that, but Paul predicted, "Evil men and impostors will grow worse and worse, deceiving and being deceived" (2 Tim. 3:13). If you haven't been persecuted yet for your faith in Jesus Christ, you will be. If you have been persecuted in the past, you can expect further persecutions.

Second, you are never given the privilege of treating others in an ungodly manner, no matter how they may mistreat you. Peter wrote, "Servants, be submissive to your masters with all fear, not only to the good and gentle, but also to the harsh" (1 Peter 2:18). Peter said you must be submissive "with all fear," which means "with all respect." It's one thing to be submissive on the outside and be hateful and vengeful on the inside. It's another thing entirely to be submissive with respect, especially to a harsh master.

Peter went on, saying,

For this is commendable, if because of conscience toward God one endures grief, suffering wrongfully. For what credit is it if, when you

are beaten for your faults, you take it patiently? But when you do good
and suffer, if you take it patiently, this is commendable before God.
For to this you were called, because Christ also suffered for us, leaving
us an example, that you should follow His steps. (1 Peter 2:19–21)

Third, nowhere in the Bible does the Lord say that obedience is easy.
Obedience makes extensive requirements of you. It requires that you
totally turn from fleshly, in-built human impulses and seek to do what
Jesus would do and say what Jesus would say. Obedience requires that
you turn from sinful habits and respond according to the nature of the
Holy Spirit who resides in you. Obedience requires that you yield daily
to the Holy Spirit so that you might manifest His character in every situation and in every relationship. You are to respond with love, joy, peace,
long-suffering (patience), kindness, goodness, faithfulness, gentleness,
and self-control (Gal. 5:22–23).

What Attitudes Are You Sowing?

The way you treat others is directly related to God's laws regarding sowing
and reaping. The apostle Paul wrote to the Galatians:

Do not be deceived, God is not mocked; for whatever a man sows, that he
will also reap. For he who sows to his flesh will of the flesh reap corruption,
but he who sows to the Spirit will of the Spirit reap everlasting life. And let
us not grow weary while doing good, for in due season we shall reap if we
do not lose heart. Therefore, as we have opportunity, let us do good to all,
especially to those who are of the household of faith. (Gal. 6:7–10)

Every morning when you and I awaken, we begin sowing. In our minds, we
sow thoughts—positive or negative, good or evil. In our actions, our
attitudes, our habits all day long, we sow either to the flesh or to the Spirit.

Every farmer knows that he cannot expect a crop unless he plants seed. Furthermore, a farmer does not expect to harvest corn if he plants wheat. He knows that what he sows is directly related to what he is going to reap, and that the *quality* of the seed he sows and the *quality* of the care with which he nurtures those seeds once they have sprouted are directly related to the *quantity* of harvest he is going to reap. The more he sows, the better quality seed he sows, and the better the farming methods used to nurture the plants produced from the seed, the greater the harvest.

God has built this principle into the natural world, the spiritual realm, the financial realm, and every other area of life. The principle has been in place from the very beginning of creation. In Genesis we read that this principle was in place even before the creation of mankind:

Then God said, "Let the earth bring forth grass, the herb that yields seed, and the fruit tree that yields fruit according to its kind, whose seed is in itself, on the earth"; and it was so. And the earth brought forth grass, the herb that yields seed according to its kind, and the tree that yields fruit, whose seed is in itself according to its kind. And God saw that it was good. (Gen. 1:11–12)

What you sow is what you reap. That law is absolutely unchangeable. And it impacts both the quantity and the nature of the harvests you receive in life as you pursue your God-given goals.

Sowing to the Flesh

Paul referred to sowing to the flesh (Gal. 6:8). Every one of us came into this world with a sinful nature, a bent away from God instead of toward Him. We are rebellious and self-willed from birth, and in countless ways, we fail to reflect the holiness and righteousness of God.

That sinful nature is in place until the day you accept Jesus Christ as your Savior. He then indwells you by the Holy Spirit and changes your sinful nature, giving you a new nature that is "of the Spirit." Your spiritual nature is altered from a state of unforgiven and sinful to forgiven and righteous before God. You truly are "born again" in your spirit. You have a fresh start. As Paul stated so well, "Therefore, if anyone is in Christ, he is a new creation; old things have passed away; behold, all things have become new" (2 Cor. 5:17).

Although your spiritual nature has changed, God does not transform your physical body. You still live in a fleshly tent, with its five senses and all of its carnality. Therefore, you still have the capacity to sin, and you can exercise your will in fulfilling the desires of the flesh.

When you choose to allow the flesh, the physical and natural-man impulses, to dominate your life, you are sowing to the flesh. Paul identified a number of fleshly sins:

Now the works of the flesh are evident, which are: adultery, fornication, uncleanness, lewdness, idolatry, sorcery, hatred, contentions, jealousies, outbursts of wrath, selfish ambitions, dissensions, heresies, envy, murders, drunkenness, revelries, and the like; of which I tell you beforehand, just as I also told you in time past, that those who practice such things will not inherit the kingdom of God. (Gal. 5:19–21)

Sowing to the flesh does not refer only to sins that we might call sexual sins or overt sins such as murder, stealing, and lying. It refers also to the way we think—hatred, jealousy, selfish ambition, heresy, envy. It refers to the way in which we relate to others—dissensions, contentions, and outbursts of wrath. We are sowing to the flesh when we retaliate against the person who wrongs us, when we lash out at the person who criticizes us, when we argue bitterly in anger with a person who disagrees with us. And the result is that we are sowing bad seed that will lead to corruption.

The things that we sow to the flesh do not produce life—rather, they produce death. The death and destruction created by our bad seed, sown to the flesh, can be vast. Consider a few of the things that a negative attitude, negative word, or negative action can kill or severely damage, especially if the negative expression is sown repeatedly:

- A loving relationship
- A good working relationship
- A marriage or family
- A business
- A ministry
- A person's physical health
- A person's mental health
- A personal testimony
- A sense of order

- Dreams
- Hopes
- Motivation
- Joy
- Contentment
- Financial blessing
- Creativity
- A will to live
- Self-esteem

Seeds sown to the flesh can result in a harvest of failures: a failure to get a promotion, a failure to make a sale, a failure to get hired, a failure to forge a positive relationship, a failure to make a new friend, a failure to keep an old friend, a failure to witness about Christ Jesus. And the list could go on and on. Nothing good can come from seeds sown to the flesh.

The person who sows to the flesh does not enjoy life. He is forever wrapped in feelings of guilt, shame, frustration, disappointment, and deep inner agitation. Only the person who sows to the Spirit has a genuine capacity to experience life at its best and its fullest.

Sowing to the Spirit

The good news is that you have a choice. You do not need to sow to the flesh, even though you live in a fleshly body with lustful impulses. You can choose to sow to the Spirit, doing things that are pleasing to the Spirit and doing them in a godly fashion. You can choose to forgive even those who have hurt you badly. You can choose to encourage those who have attempted to discourage you. You can choose to be generous toward those who have been stingy toward you. How? By allowing the Holy Spirit inside you to dominate your thinking and therefore your actions.

How do you allow the Spirit to function in you and through you to create a positive harvest for you?

First, actively submit control of your life to the Holy Spirit. You must ask the Holy Spirit on a daily basis to infuse you with His power, strength, wisdom, and ability—yielding control over your schedule, your relationships, and the use of your time, energy, and resources to Him. You can ask Him to direct you clearly into the paths in which you should walk and to give you courage to walk on those paths. Paul wrote, "If we live in the Spirit, let us also walk in the Spirit" (Gal. 5:25). In other words, it is not enough to be born again to eternal life by the power of the Holy Spirit. It is vital that you seek to walk daily on this earth in the Holy Spirit.

Second, be aware of and value the fruit that the Holy Spirit manifests in your life. You must desire to manifest love, joy, peace, patience, kindness, goodness, faithfulness, gentleness, and self-control in your life. (See Gal. 5:22–23.)

Third, actively choose what you will think about. Paul wrote to the Philippians:

Whatever things are true, whatever things are noble, whatever things are just, whatever things are pure, whatever things are lovely, whatever things are of good report, if there is any virtue and if there is anything praiseworthy—meditate on these things. (Phil. 4:8)

Choose to turn away from the negative, lustful, violent messages that swirl around you continually. Choose to turn off the television set and stay away from raunchy movies, magazines, and Internet sites. Choose to avert your eyes and ears from evil and toward good things.

What do you build up when you sow to the Spirit?

- Good friendships

- Harmonious work environments

- Active and effective ministries

- Physical and emotional health

- Loving families

- Personal joy and contentment

- Hope and enthusiasm

The things you sow in the Spirit are life producing and have the potential for eternal reward. The very nature of the Holy Spirit is *life*, and the things you sow to the Spirit produce a zest for living. They have an ability to produce, multiply, and flourish into an abundant harvest. The more you sow to the Spirit, the greater the harvest of things that result in your ability to achieve the goals that God has helped you set.

The person who has the most to gain by sowing to the Spirit is the sower. The person who has the most to lose by sowing to the flesh is also the sower. So often, we think that when we are hostile, angry, and bitter, we are causing harm to the person to whom we vent these negative emotions. In truth, we are injuring ourselves. We are destroying our inner peace, spiritual growth, Christian witness, reputation, and opportunity for reward from the Father.

I firmly believe that if you will respond in a godly fashion to a person who has hurt you, God will replace what you have lost, heal any wounds you have experienced, and prepare for you a blessing that will come in precisely the form you need it most. The person who has hurt you may not be involved in your recompense from God, but the Lord will provide for you according to His riches in glory and through His sovereign methods.

When you refuse to give in to your fleshly tendency to sow negative attitudes and behaviors, the Lord also works to build up your character, your endurance, and your faith in Him. He builds a sense of quality into your life.

Which Choice Will You Make?

Your attitudes and behaviors toward other people can be expressions of corruption, decay, and death or expressions of life.

They can be attitudes and behaviors that have a negative impact or a positive impact on your life.

They can be attitudes and behaviors that result in chaos, confusion, and loss or result in order, stability, growth, and blessing.

They can be attitudes and behaviors that result in destruction or result in the creation of good products, good service, and good relationships.

From the moment you are saved, every good work that you do, every act of service or ministry, is an act that the Lord stores up in the form of a reward for you in heaven. You can never see all of the tangible, material results of your sowing to the Spirit here on earth. Most of your rewards are going to be continuous ones that extend into eternity. You will enjoy the rewards and blessings of God *forever*!

10

SUCCESS BEGINS WITH AN IDEA

⁓

Look around. Everything you see began first with a thought. If you are looking at the natural world, every plant, skyscape, landscape, animal, insect, or body of water you see was first a thought in the mind of God. If you are looking at man-made things, every building, home, automobile, or computer was first a thought in the mind of a man or a woman. What awesome, creative power lies in the mind, the organ of thinking!

Few of us ever stop to consider fully the power of our thoughts. Most of us never really pause to question why we think the way we do or ponder the relationship between thought life and subsequent feelings, attitudes, and behaviors. The simple, obvious, but often overlooked fact is this: our thoughts today determine who we will be tomorrow. The Bible has proclaimed for thousands of years: "As he thinks in his heart, so is he" (Prov. 23:7). Your life today is the outcome of what you have thought through the years to this very moment.

How, then, are you to think in order to become the person God desires for you to be, and how are you to think as you set goals and pursue them? You are to think as Jesus thinks. Paul said to the Philippians,

"Let this mind be in you which was also in Christ Jesus" (Phil. 2:5).

In the previous chapter we talked about the importance of feeding our minds with things that are truly worthy of thought. Paul encouraged the Philippians to meditate on—to dwell on, to think about, to ponder—the things that are:

- True
- Just
- Lovely
- Virtuous
- Noble
- Pure
- Good reports
- Praiseworthy

In writing to the Colossians, Paul took a different approach. Rather than tell the Colossians what to put into their thought life, he admonished them about things they were to take out of their thought life. He said,

> Therefore put to death your members which are on the earth: fornication, uncleanness, passion, evil desire, and covetousness, which is idolatry. Because of these things the wrath of God is coming upon the sons of disobedience, in which you yourselves once walked when you lived in them. But now you yourselves are to put off all these: anger, wrath, malice, blasphemy, filthy language out of your mouth. Do not lie to one another, since you have put off the old man with his deeds, and have put on the new man who is renewed in knowledge according to the image of Him who created him. (Col. 3:5–10)

Consistently throughout his letters, Paul called us to face the fact that we are to live differently from the world, and differently from the way we lived prior to being born again. This difference is not only in what we do, but also in what we think about and how we think, which includes our opinions, beliefs, and attitudes.

Paul admonished the Colossians to put away having evil desire, covetousness, anger, wrath, and malice in the heart and mind. He knew that what we think about frequently and consistently—in other words, the thoughts we entertain—becomes behavior. Our thoughts and behavior determine our character. Our character, in turn, impacts greatly our decisions, and our decisions determine our level of success.

The mind, therefore, acts as the steering wheel for success. Where we aim our thoughts is where we generally end up, which can be at a godly destination point or in a ditch of sin and error by the side of life's highway.

When opportunities and challenges present themselves, you may say, "I need to think about this," or "I'll give this some thought." How is it, though, that you truly *think* about a decision? You think about it according to the way you have been thinking and responding to life in the past, often for many years. You make decisions according to thought patterns you have developed. Thought patterns are fueled by what you consistently take into your mind through the senses. Your thoughts are based upon what you choose to perceive. When you give your attention to something, and then fuel that attention with repeated exposure, meditation, and imagination, you end up with a well of information from which you draw thoughts.

How Do You Think About Yourself?

We especially need to consider the thoughts we have developed through the years about ourselves. Many people wake up every morning and go through their days with the abiding, nagging emotion: *I don't feel all that good about myself.* That emotion is the direct offspring of one or more of these thoughts: *I don't think I'm worthy. I don't think I'm valuable. I don't think I'm as good as the next person. I don't think my life counts. I don't think I come up to the expectations of others or the expectations I have for myself.*

The fact is, how you think or feel about yourself is going to be projected in the way you behave. It will manifest itself in the way you dress and take care of your physical appearance. It will manifest itself in your speech, usually in the form of criticism and negative comments about everything from the weather to the boss to the working environment to fellow workers. It will manifest itself in your body language—very likely a limp handshake, a slouchy walk, a dropped head, downcast eyes, a sad expression. It will manifest itself in your behavior on the job—if you don't value yourself, you aren't likely to value the work you do, and therefore, you are likely to do far less than you are capable of doing, with less quality.

In many cases, the way you think about yourself will also manifest itself in your health. Consider your first reaction when someone says to you, "You don't look very good today. Are you sick?" You probably take a look in the mirror or focus on yourself and contemplate what could be wrong. Before long, you conclude, *Well, there* must *be something wrong or that person wouldn't have said what he said,* and you start thinking and acting like a sick person. Over time, this kind of thinking really *can* result in your doing things that produce illness or, at the very minimum, produce an invalid mentality. And when people begin to treat you like a sick person or an invalid, your ability to do all that God desires for you is greatly diminished.

Can you see how your thinking relates to your success? Who wants to work with a person who is down on himself, always seems negative, and does less than superlative work? Who would want to promote such a person or give him an exciting opportunity for growth and further success? Who wants to give special benefits or rewards to a person who continually moans about feeling ill?

When you change the way you think about yourself, you very often change the circumstances around you.

Consider for a moment a person who thinks about himself, *I have a pleasing personality. I am gifted by God in unique ways. I have developed skills with God's help. I love the Lord and am accepted fully by Him as His beloved child. God is good to me—in fact, I can't wait to see what He has for me today. I have a good imagination and I am a good conversationalist. I'm good at my work and getting better all the time.*

How are you going to respond to such a person? In the first place, you likely are going to gravitate toward him because he is positive about life. If you work with this person, you are going to want to join team projects with him. If this person works for you, you are going to want to help him grow into his full potential. This person is set up for success to a great extent because of the way he thinks about himself.

The person who feels inferior is going to avoid people, and he is going to miss making the sale.

The person who is grouchy is going to turn people away, and he is going to miss out on what might have been wonderful friendships.

The person who is angry all the time is going to repel people, including those who are in a position to give promotions and raises.

The person who feels rejected and downcast is going to have a hard time witnessing to someone about the total acceptance offered by God through Jesus Christ.

What Are You Saying About Your Circumstances?

What is your first response when you walk into your kitchen or living room in the morning? Do you find yourself saying, "This place is a mess," or do you say, "I feel comfortable and totally at ease in this room"?

What is your first response when you walk into your place of employment? If you are the owner, do you find yourself saying, "I sure wish I had better employees"? If you are a worker, do you find yourself saying, "I sure wish I worked somewhere else"?

What you think about your environment—at home, on the job, in your neighborhood—will affect your behavior. It will impact the way you treat the material items around you—your possessions, your house or apartment, the equipment at work, the company's supplies.

What you think about your environment will also impact the way you talk to the people who share that environment with you—spouse, children, boss, workers, coworkers, clients, patients, vendors, students, parishioners, customers.

What Are You Thinking About Other People?

Your thoughts determine your relationships.

Do you want to get to know better the person who is always telling dirty jokes or making racial slurs?

Do you want to cultivate a friendship with a person who continually has a scowl on his face?

Do you want to share your private life with a person who is always critical of everything?

Do you want to be around a person who frequently erupts in angry outbursts?

Do you see any future in having a relationship with a person who doesn't believe what you believe about Jesus Christ?

There is an old saying that you can tell a lot about someone by the people he has chosen as friends. That's true to a great extent for this reason: people of like thinking group themselves together. People cluster around their beliefs, their mind-sets, their perspectives on life, their attitudes. It is not unusual for entire neighborhoods to reflect a consensus about politics or religion or cultural expression. Why? Because ideas result in conversation and behavior, and those who don't fit the group norm tend to move away or be ostracized.

If you are uneasy about a relationship, check your thought life. What are you thinking? How does your thinking differ from that of the other person?

What Are You Thinking About God?

Are you aware that your thoughts also determine your relationship with God? If you think of God as a judge who is keeping score continually about your behavior and judging you guilty and unworthy at every turn, are you really going to want to spend time with God in prayer and quiet meditation on His Word?

On the other hand, if you think of God as a loving Father, you are much more likely to desire to spend time reading His Word and communicating with Him.

What you think about God will impact your relationship with the church as well. If you regard Jesus Christ as the head of the church, and you think of the church as the body of Christ, you are going to have a relationship with the church that is much different from the one you will have if you think about the church as a social club to which you belong.

If you made a list today of ten words that describe how you think about yourself, what words would you choose? Write them on a sheet of paper that only you will see.

What is your thought profile of yourself?

Now write a list of ten words that describe how you think about God.

In all likelihood, you are going to see a definite relationship between the two lists. The person who has a positive thought profile of God usually has a positive thought profile of himself. The person who feels down about himself tends to feel negative about God.

Check your thoughts! They are directly related to your faith.

What Are You Thinking About
Your Family and Children?

The way you think about your spouse is the way you will treat your spouse. If you think your spouse is unworthy of your love and affection, a disappointment, a lazy slob, or a vain braggart, you are going to treat your spouse accordingly, usually with rejection, disdain, condescension, anger, or a lack of forgiveness. Your behavior is going to drive a wedge between you and your spouse.

On the other hand, if you think your spouse is a gift of God to you, a wonderful beloved child of God who is developing and growing according to God's plan, and a person who makes mistakes but is trying to overcome them, you are going to treat your spouse with much greater kindness, generosity, affection, acceptance, and forgiveness.

Which category of attitudes and behavior do you want to live with in your marriage?

The same principle holds true for your relationship with your children. How you think about a child results in the way you speak to that child, what you give to that child, and how you treat that child.

My stepfather made it very clear to me what he thought of me: I was worthless, an annoyance, an unwanted presence. He never said a positive, uplifting word to me, gave me anything, or chose to spend time with me. The result? We had no relationship. It is a sad fact of my childhood, but a fact nonetheless.

How we think about one another in the family results in our very definition of the family: whether we are close-knit or distant as a family, caring or indifferent, loving or hateful, a joy or a stressful obligation.

Ask yourself often, What kind of thoughts am I planting in my child's mind about himself, about me as a parent, and about our family? A survey of prisoners revealed that the vast majority of them had been told at some point in their lives by their parents, "You'll probably end up in prison one of these days."

Choose to plant positive, upward-thinking, faith-building thoughts in your child's mind. Tell your child of God's love for him and the wonderful and purposeful future God has planned for him. Tell him about God's plan for your family and about your belief that God loves you, your child, and each member of your family with an unfathomable, immeasurable, unconditional love.

The Limitations of Positive Thinking

You may be saying, "Well, Dr. Stanley, are you advocating positive thinking—the idea that positive thoughts and a positive attitude will automatically result in positive rewards and success?" No—and let me explain why I don't believe that positive thinking automatically produces success.

First, positive thinking must always be rooted in what God says about you, not in what you say about yourself. You can look in a mirror and say, "I'm the greatest," one hundred times a day every day for the rest of your life, yet not be successful in achieving God's goals for your life. Why? Because you are trying to pump yourself up in your attitude according to what you think, not according to the Word of God. On the other hand, if you remind yourself and are truly convinced of God's truth that God loves you, God has equipped you with specific skills and abilities, and God is present always to help you in every circumstance, what you say to yourself and what you say about yourself to others are going to be rooted in truth. And that truth is a forerunner of successful behavior.

Second, positive thinking must be linked to positive behavior for success to be the outcome. Positive behavior is diligent, honest, truthful, loving, kind, generous, persistent, and joyful. You can think you are wonderful—even righteously so—but if you fail to work, or to do what the Lord has put before you to do, you will never succeed.

A man can stare at a piece of ground all day and say or think every five minutes, *I'm a child of God and a skilled ditchdigger,* but if that man doesn't pick up a shovel and start digging ditches, no ditch is going to be made, and he isn't going to be paid for his work.

Third, positive thinking is never to become justification for harboring or failing to confront sin and evil. You need to be able to separate your thoughts about a deed that someone does from your thoughts about the person who is doing the deed. It is very possible to love the sinner and hate the sin.

Again, the apostle Paul is a good example. Paul seemed continually to be in a confrontational stance against evil. Everywhere he went, he suffered persecution for standing up for the gospel against those who opposed it. He spoke out strongly against sin. Yet Paul loved people deeply. In his letters, he wrote to the believers as his beloved children in the Lord, and he encouraged them continually to love one another and serve one another. You can be opposed to sin and at the same time love those who persecute you, ridicule you, criticize you, or hurt you.

Given these limitations, however, you must also conclude the following:

- Positive thinking that is rooted in what God says about a person can be extremely powerful and effective.

- Positive thinking is a great motivator toward positive behavior. A person is much more likely to behave in positive ways if he first thinks positive thoughts.

- Positive thinking must always be the way you think about a person's future, including your own future in the Lord. Jesus taught that we must always hold out the hope of redemption for another person, regardless of behavior. He said, "Judge not, and you shall not be judged. Condemn not, and you shall not be condemned. Forgive, and you will be forgiven" (Luke 6:37). You are not to think of any person as being beyond the reach of God's everlasting arms, mercy, and forgiveness.

God's Challenge to Think Positively

Is a negative response to the life God sets before you ever warranted?
No.
Of all the people we encounter in the New Testament, the apostle Paul

probably had the greatest reason to develop negative thinking. He encountered a host of negative situations and responses to his preaching of the gospel.
He spent the last years of his life in confinement, most of that time chained
to Roman guards. Did Paul have a negative mind-set? Read what he wrote to
the Philippians from his prison chamber in Rome:

> I rejoiced in the Lord greatly that now at last your care for me has flour-
> ished again; though you surely did care, but you lacked opportunity. Not
> that I speak in regard to need, for I have learned in whatever state I am,
> to be content: I know how to be abased, and I know how to abound.
> Everywhere and in all things I have learned both to be full and to be hun-
> gry, both to abound and to suffer need. I can do all things through Christ
> who strengthens me . . . I am full, having received from Epaphroditus the
> things sent from you, a sweet-smelling aroma, an acceptable sacrifice,
> well pleasing to God. And my God shall supply all your need according
> to His riches in glory by Christ Jesus. (Phil. 4:10–13, 18–19)

Paul was in prison, yet he wrote with an attitude of thanksgiving,
encouragement, contentment, and faith in the Lord to supply not only his
needs, but also the needs of the Philippians. Paul chose to think God's
way—that adversity does not mean defeat—and to believe for God's highest and best at all times. He chose to think in terms of godly success.

Paul chose to focus on the good opportunities that were around him
and that he believed were still ahead of him. He didn't write to the
Philippians about how cold or dark or damp his prison chamber might be
from time to time. He didn't write about all the things he missed or about
the things he wished he could have. He didn't write to them about how
unfair the accusations against him had been or about facing his death. No!
He wrote a life-giving, joyful, and faith-filled letter.

Was Paul an idealist or a fantasizer? No. He was a realist. He didn't deny
that he faced problems or that he was in prison. Paul recognized, as we

must, that life is never totally negative or totally positive. We can choose which side of life to think about, to believe for, and to aim at.

The Programming and Reprogramming of Your Mind

Many people make decisions to change something about their lives, very often as a part of New Year's resolutions. Then they are disappointed in themselves when they realize that they aren't keeping their resolutions one week, two weeks, or a month later.

Why do we find it so difficult to keep our resolutions to change our behavior? Because we haven't made a more basic decision to change the thinking habits we have developed through the years. As I stated previously, our attitudes and thoughts generate our actions. They determine our behavior. That is a basic law that God has built into human nature, and we cannot change His laws about human nature. We can, however, change our thinking habits and put into motion a new cycle of thinking and behaving. The will overrides thoughts. We can choose to think new thoughts and, in turn, behave in new ways.

If you don't like the way you are living right now, or if you don't like the direction in which your life seems to be moving, take a look at your thought life. Take a look at your thought patterns. You can choose to make a change for the better and toward God in the way you think. You can make a choice for success.

At the Root Is Faith

You may be saying, "Dr. Stanley, are you advocating mind over matter? Are you saying that if I just think positively, things will become positive?" No. Positive thoughts alone are not enough.

To a great extent, mind *is* over matter. What you think gives you rulership over the material world. But the greater fact is this: *spirit is to be over mind.* Your spirit should govern what you choose to think about and, therefore, how you choose to relate to the material world. Your faith must be at the root of your ideas, goals, dreams, aspirations, and hopes. The mind then takes those faith-born ideas, goals, and dreams and develops them into plans, schedules, and agendas. And as you execute your plans and schedules and agendas, you impact the material world around you. The beginning point is not mind over matter, but spirit over mind!

Line Up Your Thinking with God's Word and Love

Many of us need to reprogram our thinking to line up with God's Word and God's love for us.

Years ago, a woman in my church told me, "When I was growing up, my daddy said to me, 'Honey, you are as good as the rest, and you're better than the best.'" This tall, dignified, beautiful woman was in her eighties when she said that to me, and she was as confident as she could be. I could tell that she had never forgotten and would never forget what her daddy had told her. He had programmed her thinking well.

We have been programmed in our thinking by somebody. Our parents, our teachers, our pastors and Sunday school teachers through the years, our friends, and even our enemies have programmed things into our thinking. The media and the general opinions and conversations we hear and over-hear in our society program our thinking. How many people buy products based upon what they have heard on the radio or seen on television?

Some of the ways in which you have been programmed have been and continue to be good. Other ways in which you have been programmed are bad. It is up to you, as an adult who is responsible for your own life, to make decisions about both past and current programming of your thoughts. You need to take charge of your thought life. You are extremely unwise if you continue to say, "Well, that's just the way my parents raised me," or "That's just the way everybody thinks."

The fact is, some of the ways in which you have been programmed to think are *not* pleasing to God. Some of your thoughts and opinions do not line up with God's thoughts and opinions of you. Some of the ways in which you continue to program your mind are not the way God desires for you to think.

Paul wrote to the Romans:

I beseech you therefore, brethren, by the mercies of God, that you present your bodies a living sacrifice, holy, acceptable to God, which is your reasonable service. And do not be conformed to this world, but be transformed by the renewing of your mind, that you may prove what is that good and acceptable and perfect will of God. (Rom. 12:1–2)

The transformation of your mind to be conformed to the things of God is your responsibility—nobody else's. It is your responsibility to *prove* what is good and acceptable before God, and to know and live out the perfect will of God. Paul said very clearly, "Stop allowing yourself to be poured into the world's mold."

The Greek word for "renewing" the mind is a word that means "make a change." To renew the mind is literally to change the way you think.

Think back for a moment to the way you lived before you were born again. Even if you were born again as a child, you can no doubt recall certain attitudes and beliefs. Nearly every person can recall having some degree of fear or dread about God prior to being saved. Most people can recall having doubts, anger, or impure or self-justifying thoughts. All of these ways of thinking, Paul said, must go. You must change the way you think about God and yourself and your neighbors so that you no longer think thoughts that are rooted in fear, apprehension about God, doubt, anger, impurity, or self-justification. You must experience a *transformation* in your thinking habits.

"But," you may say, "I think just the way I used to think. There's no difference in the way I thought before I was saved and the way I think now." Friend, I encourage you to reevaluate your salvation experience. The Christian life demands a way of thinking that is distinctly different from the way the world thinks. The longer you live the Christian life, the more you will understand God, yourself, and others, and the more you will be challenged to make even more changes in your thinking.

What You Can Do to Reprogram Your Thinking

You have the God-given power to do several things to improve your thought life so that your thoughts line up with God's thinking about you and His plans for you.

First, you can choose to reject thoughts that are sinful and, therefore, imprisoning to your mind. You can refuse to think about or dwell upon things that put you in spiritual bondage. You can reject thoughts that steal your freedom and your dreams of pursuing God's plan for your life.

You cannot avoid some impulses and images. Your eyes will spot things that are unrighteous. You will overhear things that are evil. You will find yourself in situations against your will that are unpleasant and sinful. But you do not need to remain in these situations, and you do not need to dwell upon the evil things you see and hear.

Take action immediately. Turn your eyes away. Close your ears. Change channels. Toss the magazine into the trash. Get away. Excuse yourself and leave the room. Do not remain in the environment where evil presses in on your senses.

No person can control completely the thoughts that fly into his mind. But a person can take charge over those thoughts. A person has a choice to say, "I refuse to think about that," or "I'm not going to ponder that." It isn't a sin to think a lustful, hateful, or dishonest thought, but it *is* a sin to willfully entertain the thought, embellish it, dwell on it, or act on it.

Ask the Lord immediately to cleanse you of what you have seen, heard, or experienced. Ask the Lord to help you wipe all memory of that moment or experience from your mind so that it will have no bearing on your future conversations or behavior.

And then refuse to talk about the evil that you have encountered. In talking about what you have experienced, you are reinforcing that idea to your mind, and you are spreading the evil to a person who didn't encounter it. Don't repeat the off-color joke, the negative remark, the critical gossip, the potentially damaging rumor.

Finally, do not recall the experience. Do not allow yourself to fantasize or dwell upon the images you saw, the things you heard, or the feelings you had. You have the ability to *choose* what you will think about—exercise that privilege God has given you.

Second, you can immerse yourself in the Word of God. The psalmist announced,

> Your Word I have hidden in my heart,
> That I might not sin against You. (Ps. 119:11)

The more you read, study, reflect upon, and memorize God's Word, the more your thoughts are going to line up with the truth of God's Word.

You must have a daily "thought diet" of God's Word. Reading the Word of God at least once a day is not just a good idea, it's the *best* idea and habit you can develop when it comes to renewing your mind.

The more you read God's Word, the more you will discover that it is filled with "success thoughts." All of the principles of genuine success come from the Word of God. The Bible is the most positive and success-oriented book you can read. The Bible will teach you, by direct instruction and by the examples of men and women through the centuries, how to develop the traits necessary for success: generosity, discipline, wisdom, discernment, righteous living, faith, diligent work, a readiness to listen to God, courage, and persistence.

The Bible tells you directly what you need to *stop* doing: "Put off all these: anger, wrath, malice, blasphemy, filthy language . . . Do not lie to one another" (Col. 3:8–9). The Bible also tells you what to *start* doing:

"Put on tender mercies, kindness, humility, meekness, longsuffering; bearing with one another, and forgiving one another" (Col. 3:12–13).

The Bible conveys practical ways of surviving difficulty and hardship. It teaches you how to relate to the heavenly Father and to others. It teaches you how to act in kindness and gentleness. It teaches you how to develop a servant's spirit and how to discover God's purpose for your life. All of these things are directly associated with success.

Third, you must spend time with the Lord every day. In your prayer life, you must develop an ability to listen to the Lord, not just make your petitions to the Lord. You must also listen to what you are saying to the Lord. What are you asking for? What are you saying to the Lord about yourself? Are your prayers couched in terms of praise and thanksgiving? Do you approach the Lord with a positive, faith-filled attitude?

Ask the Lord to help you in the renewal of your mind. Ask Him to recall His Word to you at just the times you need it. Invite the Lord to have a say in every decision you make.

Fourth, you must start thanking the Lord for the positive thoughts and attitudes that you desire to develop in your life.

All through my growing-up years, I never seriously allowed the truth that God loved me to enter my mind. I thought of God as a judge. I believed He had provided a Savior for me in Jesus Christ, and I believed in Jesus. I believed that God would take care of me and provide for me and help me. But love me? That was a foreign thought to me.

It was not until I was an adult, through a series of experiences, that I came to a deep, inner realization that God truly loved me—infinitely, unconditionally, tenderly, and completely. I had preached God's love for years, but I had not really programmed my mind to know God's love and to think and respond to life from a perspective of a beloved child of God.

How did I retrain my thinking? I went to bed at night saying, "Lord, I thank You for loving me." When I'd awaken in the morning, I'd say, "Lord,

I thank You for loving me." Did I always feel God's love as I said these words? No. But I knew that they were true words, I knew that God's love for me was real and true, and I knew that a thought pattern of God's love was a good and true pattern to have.

I persisted in repeating this statement, and over time, the most amazing thing happened. I began to feel God's love. I began to feel wrapped up in His love from head to toe, all day long. I began to think, speak, and respond to life as a person loved by God. My attitudes began to be infused with God's love. My words and my behaviors became more loving. I truly began to live in freedom from the terrible bondage of wrong thinking about God as a severe judge and distant observer of my life.

Do I still say every night and every morning, "Lord, I thank You for loving me"? No. Some nights and some mornings I do. But I no longer need to develop this thought pattern. It is established. I live in it. I respond to life from the perspective of a person who knows he is loved beyond measure.

Is this self-hypnosis or self-definition? No. It's renewing the mind so that your thinking is in line with God's truth. It is replacing the negative programming of the past. It is establishing truth in the place of error. It is speaking to your mind what *God* says rather than what the devil has been saying to you for years.

I know a man who was an outright gangster as a youth. It would be hard to name too many bad things that he didn't do as a young man. He was totally warped and bent in one direction—toward hell. Where did the turnaround in this man's life begin? In his thinking. One day he began to think, *If I continue to live the way I'm living, I'm going to end up like all my buddies, dead and in hell.* He began to think about what it would be like to burn in hell. And he made a change that began with this thought: *I don't want to live like I've been living.*

Then this man began to think, *Could God change me? Could God love me and forgive me?* The more he went to church and the more he read God's Word, the more he became convinced that God could forgive him and change him. He turned toward God, and through the years, he has been intent upon the renewal of his mind so that he thinks today as God thinks, and he chooses to act as God desires for him to act. His life has been transformed completely—it has been a transformation that began in his thinking.

The world advocates a form of renewal for the mind called *autosuggestion*. That is, a person suggests things to himself. I believe instead in *God commandments*. Every day as I read God's Word I look for the things that God tells me to do, including how to think. I look for the directives of God that are related to my beliefs, attitudes, feelings, responses, and behavior. These are the things I want to say to myself: "God says to me, 'Charles Stanley, I love you'"; "God says to me, 'Charles Stanley, I want you to forgive that person who wronged you'"; "God says to me, 'Charles Stanley, I want you to have boldness and courage as you take on this spiritual battle.'"

If I fill my mind with what God says, I fill my mind with truth. I fill my mind with goodness—in fact, with the absolute goodness of God's presence and love. I do not suggest things to myself that I might hope for in the flesh. Rather, I speak God's commandments to myself.

A Christian's priority must always be to know God and to walk in His ways. I always look for something about the Lord that I don't know or haven't understood. I always look for His direct commandments to *me*.

When you allow truth to dominate your mind, you will truly begin to walk in the ways the Holy Spirit wants you to walk. Ask the Lord today to give you a right understanding of the following:

- Money and finances
- Marriage
- Family
- Business
- Ministry

- Friendships
- Material possessions
- Self—your abilities, capacities, and dreams

Ask the Lord today to give you clear thinking about the decisions you face. Ask the Lord today to give you *His* ideas and creativity.

Fifth, you can take preemptive action by choosing to become involved in positive relationships and activities. Choose to affiliate with individuals and groups that display good character and righteousness before God.

Get involved in a Bible study, a home fellowship group, or an outreach ministry instead of plopping down on the sofa for a night of prime-time violence and off-color jokes. Go to church instead of the local club or bar. Choose to do what is positive. You have the power to make decisions about how you will spend your time, money, and mental energy. As Paul wrote to the Colossians, "Set your minds on things above, not on things on the earth" (Col. 3:2).

At any given moment in a situation, you can choose to redirect your thoughts to what you have read in God's Word. Close your eyes, and focus your spiritual eyesight on Jesus. As the old gospel song says so well, "The things of earth will grow strangely dim in the light of His glory and grace."

Sixth, you can ask the Lord to help you monitor your speech. Many people are in the habit of saying negative things about themselves and others. They no longer recognize what they are doing or what they are reinforcing in their minds. Listen closely to yourself!

The person who is most influenced by negative comments is the person who makes those comments. Your ears are usually the ears closest to the words coming out of your mouth. Don't become a victim of your own negative recycled speaking.

Anytime you hear yourself say something negative, downgrading, critical, or harsh about yourself or any other person, immediately take these steps. Ask the Lord to forgive you for belittling or diminishing the value of a person He created and loves infinitely, including yourself. Immediately say something positive about yourself or the other person; find something to compliment genuinely or something to praise. Thank the Lord for His work being done in you or the other person. Acknowledge that each of us is a work in progress and that the Lord is present and active in your life and the lives of others.

Seventh, at the end of the day, you can ask God to cleanse you of any anger, bitterness, or evil thoughts that you have allowed to take root in your mind. People may say, "Well, I'm going to forget about this tonight and get some sleep. I'll think about it in the morning." They awaken the next morning to discover they didn't sleep well. All night long the subconscious mind was dwelling on the thoughts that they were holding on to until the morning. Ask the Lord to give you peace at night, to help you forgive and let go of the anxieties, troubles, hurts, and struggles of the day. Ask Him to fill your mind with thoughts of His goodness toward you. Develop this as a daily habit and you'll probably be surprised at how well you begin to sleep and how refreshed you feel when you awaken each day.

I often pray as I go to bed, "Lord, I want to thank You for today. I ask You to take control of my subconscious mind as I sleep and to allow the Holy Spirit to continue to work in me even through the night hours. You know the things that I need and the ideas that I must have in order to do the work You have called me to do. I ask You to begin the birthing process of those ideas even as I sleep."

I am often amazed that the first thoughts I have upon awaking are creative ideas that are just what I needed for a particular sermon or for a particular project or decision facing me. They are ideas birthed in the peace of the Lord and in total submission of my thinking to the Holy Spirit.

At times now, the Lord will awaken me at two-thirty in the morning with an idea that is crystal clear to me. In those moments, I write down that idea immediately, and then I go back to sleep. I'm not only grateful for the idea, but I also have discovered that those interruptions to my sleep don't leave me feeling exhausted.

In contrast, if I allow myself to go to bed troubled about something, my mind continues to churn on that topic while my body is trying to sleep. If I awaken in the middle of the night, I rarely have an answer—my mind is still dwelling on the problem. And the more I think about the problem in the middle of the night, the more troubled my mind can become. Rarely do I feel refreshed and thoroughly rested after such a night.

When you are facing a question, problem, major decision, or challenge, ask God to think it through for you. Present that problem to the Lord before you go to sleep, and say to the Lord, "I'm giving this to You tonight. Help me to sleep soundly and peacefully, knowing that You are in control of all the situations and circumstances of my life, including this problem. I thank You in advance for the solution You are going to reveal. I thank You for creating my body for work and for rest. I thank You for creating my mind for making decisions and developing ideas under the guidance of the Holy Spirit. I yield myself to You fully tonight."

Invite the Lord to arrange and rearrange the sensory input and the information in your mind as you sleep. Ask Him to produce in you *His* thoughts, *His* ideas, and *His* creativity. When you awaken, look for the answers the Lord may have given you in the night.

Create a New Cycle

We all know people who have become hooked on certain things. It may be pornography, illicit and immoral sexual behavior, alcohol, or drugs. Where did those addictions begin? In their minds. They saw something, heard something, or experienced a foretaste of something, and they began to think about it. They fantasized about it. They wondered what even more of that substance or experience might be like. They daydreamed and imagined themselves engaged in more and more of the behavior they had tried. And their thinking directed their behavior. The more they engaged in the behavior they had been thinking about, the more they thought about their own behavior, and the cycle of thinking and behaving intensified and became more routine until they were addicted.

The cycle can be reversed. You can choose to focus your thinking on the things of heaven and engage in acts of ministry and behaviors that build your relationship with the Lord. The more you engage in these ministries and godly behaviors, the more your imagination will be triggered to think, *What more can I be doing for the Lord?* And the more you seek to answer this question, the more involved you will be in the pursuit of things that are rooted in righteousness. A positive thinking and behaving cycle can be established.

Years ago, I came across this little poem. I share it with you as a final word of encouragement to use your faith and will to take charge of your thought life:

If you think you're beaten, you are.
If you think you dare not, you don't.
If you like to win, but you think you can't, it is almost certain
    you won't.
If you think you'll lose, you've lost.

For out in the world we find success begins with a fellow's will.
It's all in the state of mind.
If you think you're outclassed, you are.
You've got to think high to rise.

You've got to be sure of yourself before you can ever win a prize.
Life's battles don't always go to the stronger or faster man,
But sooner or later the man who wins is the man who thinks he can.

11

THE SUCCESSFUL USE OF TIME

~⌒

You cannot separate success from a wise use of time. Many people attempt to be successful without giving any thought to time, but those who truly attain success have learned to respect and honor time in their lives.

The apostle Paul had this to say about time management: "See then that you walk circumspectly, not as fools but as wise, redeeming the time, because the days are evil" (Eph. 5:15–16).

To "walk circumspectly" is to be careful in the way one lives. Paul identified two general lifestyles: foolish and wise. Those who seek to live in wisdom use time wisely. They don't discount minutes and hours, or think only in terms of days and years. They have learned a key principle for success: *moments are important.*

To the Galatians, Paul wrote, "Let us not grow weary while doing good . . . As we have opportunity, let us do good to all" (Gal. 6:9–10). The Greek word for "opportunity" means "making the most of your time." Time and opportunity are vitally linked to success.

I personally do not know a genuinely successful person who is indifferent about the use of time and the schedule he keeps. A successful person seeks to get the most value out of every minute, hour, and day.

Time: A Precious Gift from God

Time is God-given. Life is simply a span of time that God has given to each of us—a segment of moments carved out of eternity in which we are to live on this earth and fulfill the plan and purpose God has for our lives. The psalmist wrote,

> Your eyes saw my substance, being yet unformed.
> And in Your book they all were written,
> The days fashioned for me,
> When as yet there were none of them. (Ps. 139:16)

An equally important point for us to grasp is that we don't know the fullness of the time span allotted to us. We know only that it is appointed to man to die—an appointment time has been set.

In addition to time being a gift and an unknown quantity, time is irrevocable. We cannot capture minutes that are lost and relive them in a way that is more meaningful or purposeful. There have been times in my life when I have gone to the barbershop and after looking at how short the barber cut my hair, I wanted to say, "Put some hair back on!" But once you have had your hair cut, glue can't reattach it. The same is true for time.

I can't pray today what I should have prayed yesterday. I can't do yesterday's reading of my Bible today. I can't go back and attend the church service I should have attended. Once a second has ticked by, it's gone. There is no recapturing it.

You can't give me any of your time; I can't loan you some of mine. I can't relive any hours of my life and neither can you. We can use time and waste time, but we cannot store up time or relive time.

Knowing that time is God's gift to you, time is irrevocable, and your life span is undisclosed to you should lead you to value time greatly. If you have no time left, you have no life left!

None of us know where we are on God's timetable for the ages. But we do know that time is running out on this world. Jesus is coming back, and God is going to wrap up His plan for this age. We don't know when Jesus is returning, any more than we know the length of our God-given days on this earth. But we do know that we are one day closer today to the Lord's return than we were yesterday. And we do know that the Lord tells us to watch for the Lord's return and to be diligent in our efforts to win souls and build up the body of Christ as we watch. Romans 14:10 admonishes us, "We shall all stand before the judgment seat of Christ." The day is coming when we will make an accounting to the Lord for how we have spent our time.

Therefore, in the light of these characteristics of time, the question you must ask is this: How can I use my talents and gifts from God in the time I have received from God in order to fulfill my purpose from God? It is not enough to have goals and gifts. You must put the goals and gifts to work in the context of time.

An Urgency About Time

Throughout the Bible, we find references to the brevity of life and the swift movement of our lives through time. Job declared, "My days are swifter than a weaver's shuttle" (Job 7:6).

When I was in college, I worked summers in a textile mill. The shuttles of the looms moved back and forth so fast, a person could hardly watch them. Certainly they didn't move that quickly in Job's time, but nonetheless, Job could see the seconds of his life ticking away just as a weaver's shuttle moves back and forth across a loom.

James wrote, "What is your life? It is even a vapor that appears for a little time and then vanishes away" (James 4:14). We have so little time, and yet from God's perspective, we have just the right amount of time to do what He has ordained for us to do.

Rather than be discouraged about the brevity of life, you need to be challenged to come to grips with time. You cannot extend your days, but you can determine to a great extent the quality and productivity of your life. You can determine your attitude toward time and make decisions related to your use of it. You can seek to be a good and faithful steward of all that God has given to you, including time.

The Erratic Dimension of Time

As much as you can seek to control your schedule, you also must acknowledge that you cannot fully control time. Life has incidents, situations, and circumstances that are beyond your personal control. For example, a mother may have her day well planned for activities that she truly believes are fulfilling God's purpose for her life, only to receive a call from her child's school that her child is ill and she needs to pick him up and care for him.

In moments when your plans are interrupted by circumstances beyond your control, you must be flexible, regroup quickly, and move to Plan B. There are a million things that can be done with an hour. Choose something that is worthy, valuable, and good in the eyes of the Lord.

What Is a Waste of Time?

Wasting time is a sin. But we must recognize that God is the One who defines what is a waste. He defines a waste of time as anything that does not contribute to the fulfillment of His plan and purpose for us.

Are recreation and play wastes of time? Not necessarily. God intends for you to rest and to relax and to have moments of pure enjoyment. That's a part of His plan for the rejuvenation of your body, mind, and spirit.

Is spending time alone, listening to the Lord and quietly waiting in His presence, a waste of time? No. God delights in having fellowship with you. Setting aside time alone with the Lord is a vital way of building a relationship with the Lord and of coming to hear clearly what the Lord desires for you to do with your time and energy.

Are prayer and conversations about God wastes of time? Never! If you are sitting in traffic, doing a menial task, or waiting for an appointment, use that time to talk to God or to strike up a conversation about the love of God.

Are reading and studying wastes of time? No. Not if you are reading or studying something that is valuable to the fulfillment of your God-given goals. You develop talents and gifts from God by studying. Studying is not a waste of time if you are studying the right things for the right reasons.

But playing when you should be working, sleeping when you should be awake, or spending time doing frivolous things at the expense of spending time with the Lord or family and friends—that is a waste.

Is it a waste of time to be a workaholic and spend eighteen hours a day, seven days a week, on a job or a career or a ministry? Yes. Eventually that schedule is going to lead to burnout. Furthermore, it is to live in disobedience to God's commandment: "Six days you shall labor and do all your work, but the seventh day is the Sabbath of the LORD your God" (Ex. 20:9–10). To work continually is not a balanced approach to time; a person's physical strength and energy are sapped over the long haul, the person's relationships with God, family, and friends—relationships that are very important in God's plan for everyone—are weakened.

Nothing is a waste of time if it is part of a balanced plan for time—a plan developed for the fulfillment of God's purposes and for maximum usefulness, productivity, and efficiency in the use of your talents and gifts.

What Drives Your Use of Time?

Many people allow their days to be driven by external circumstances. They do what unfolds before them moment by moment. To a great extent, they allow others to dictate their use of time. They yield to every demand placed upon them by others. They go through their days saying, "He wants me to do this, she wants me to attend that, he wants me to go there, and she wants me to finish this." These people react to the time demands of others. In the end, they can be very busy and, at times, productive—but not in the ways the Lord has intended for them to be busy and productive. They are fulfilling the wishes of others, not the purposes of God for their lives.

Others are driven by their desires. They have a desire to rest, so they sit down, and before they know it, they have watched three hours of television, very little of which matters to their lives and the vast majority of which they cannot remember several days later. Others are driven by their cravings for alcohol or drugs or food. Others are driven by a desire for material possessions and money—they pursue shopping and investing with a vengeance in order to satisfy a deep unmet longing. And still others are driven by unfulfilled restlessness that compels them to be with people and to be busy in "fun" activities from morning until evening.

For the most part, those who allow their desires to drive their use of time have not faced the real deep needs and purposes of their lives. They live on the surface of their emotions, seeking to satisfy something that cannot be satisfied by substances, possessions, activities, or other people.

Rarely have I met a person who was driven by a deep desire to read the Bible, pray, attend church, or share his faith with others. Those who are driven by desire in their use of time are usually driven in directions away from godly disciplines and events.

In contrast are those who choose to manage their time according to what they know is pleasing to God. In essence, they are not dictating their schedules. Rather, they are yielding their time to the Lord and asking Him for *His* schedule. Then they are managing what *He* has directed them to do within a given time—it may be an hour, a day, a week.

Value What Is Important

You must recognize that many things in life are urgent but not important. Circumstances, the demands of others, and your unfulfilled desires create a sense of urgency, but rarely are these things rooted in the real importance of the God-given goals for you. Keep your eyes focused on what is important.

Do you value your relationship with God? If so, you are going to spend time with Him.

Do you value the Word of God? If so, you are going to spend time reading it.

Do you value the talents that God has given you? If so, you are going to spend time developing them and using them wisely.

Every week as I prepare my Sunday sermon, I approach my work with a sense of value. I value the privilege of preaching the gospel. I value the privilege of ministering to those in my church and to those who hear my sermons by means of radio and television around the world. I value the people who are seeking to grow in their relationship with the Lord. I value the call of God on my life to share the love and forgiveness of Jesus Christ with others.

Because I value the opportunity to preach, I spend an average of twenty hours a week in sermon preparation, not including the countless hours I am thinking and praying about my next sermon.

How do you approach your work or your ministry? Do you value what you do?

How do you approach your family and friends? Do you value their presence in your life?

Hindrances to Managing Time

There are three basic hindrances to good time management. The first is *misplaced priorities.*

What are your priorities? What matters most to you? I suggest you write down your top four priorities. Then take a look at your schedule for tomorrow in light of those priorities. Are you actually doing things that reflect your priorities?

Many people have as a priority, "Grow in my relationship with the Lord," and yet a look at their schedules reveals they have pitifully few moments designated for activities that will nurture their relationship with their heavenly Father. If you truly value your relationship with the Lord and have made it a priority for your life, designate time every day to read and study God's Word, to pray, and to be involved in encouraging others in their faith walk.

I know several people who spend hours every day on the telephone. Most of that time, however, is spent in idle chatter: "Hi, howya doing?" "Fine." "Whatcha been up to?" "Nothin' much." Millions of calls a day are made across this nation and around the world in which the caller didn't have a real reason for calling. Have a reason for what you do! Make that reason the doing of something you have designated as a priority.

A second major hindrance to good time management is *procrastination*. Procrastinators never get anywhere in life. They are always in "delay" mode.

Most procrastinators have wonderful intentions, they may have good priorities, and they may even set schedules and agendas that reflect those priorities. They just never get around to doing what they have planned to do.

A number of years ago a pastor attended one of our administrative conferences in downtown Atlanta, and he told me, "I go into my study at eight o'clock in the morning, expecting to have a profitable day, and then I look up from my desk and see that a book is out of place on my bookshelf, so I get up and put it in its place. Then I see that some papers need to be straightened and some pencils need to be sharpened, and before I know it, I have spent four hours doing one little unnecessary thing after another. In all that time, I haven't opened my Bible, spent time on my knees, or written a word." This man had done everything but his priorities—a classic sign of procrastination.

A third hindrance to good time management is a *lack of concentration*. Concentration involves setting your mind on a particular subject or project and staying there until you understand the subject or complete the project. It takes concentration to produce quality work, to engage in quality practice as you develop a talent or skill, or to learn something in such a way that the information stays with you. If you don't develop an ability to focus your attention and concentrate on a task at hand, you cannot make the most of your time.

Oh, you may spend an hour with a Bible in your lap, staring at a page and reading a particular verse over and over again, while your mind meanders to a dozen other concerns. That's not going to be a genuinely productive, valuable hour of Bible study. You have not made good use of that hour.

You may spend eight hours at work, but do you perform eight hours *of* work? Or do you allow yourself to be distracted continually?

Multitasking—doing two or more tasks in the same time period—may be a popular concept today, but most successful people I know do one thing at a time with their full concentration. They stay organized as they go, keeping all aspects of a project together and leaving that project only when they are at a well-defined stopping point. If they are meeting with a person—face-to-face or on the phone—they give that person their full concentration. If they are writing, they write without interruption. If they are working at a project with their hands, they complete the project without distraction. Stay focused. Concentrate!

Misplaced priorities, procrastination, and a lack of concentration truly can lead you to waste time. You accomplish nothing that matters.

Seven Keys to Good Time Management

The Bible gives us seven keys for good time management. They call for us to take charge of our schedules and agendas, to base the use of our time upon what is truly important to God, and to adjust our schedules according to the priorities, plans, and purposes that the Lord gives to us for each day of our lives.

Key #1: Assume Responsibility

The first key is assuming responsibility for your use of time. The Bible challenges us to redeem the time, which means to make the most of the time God has given us. (See Eph. 5:16.) Choose to take charge of your time to the best of your ability. If you don't manage your time, somebody else will.

Key #2: Seek God's Guidance

Recognize that God has ordained for you a series of good works to accomplish. We read in Ephesians 2:10, "We are His workmanship, created in Christ Jesus for good works, which God prepared beforehand that we should walk in them."

Peter had this to say about a person's management of time:

He no longer should live the rest of his time in the flesh for the lusts of men, but for the will of God. For we have spent enough of our past lifetime in doing the will of the Gentiles . . . As each one has received a gift, minister it to one another, as good stewards of the manifold grace of God. (1 Peter 4:2–3, 10)

Ask the Lord each morning to help you identify the good works that He has planned for you on that particular day. Ask the Lord to show you *how* and *when* and *to whom* you might minister by using the good gifts and talents that He has given you.

Don't limit your petition for God's guidance to the time you spend at work or in ministry. Ask the Lord to help you manage your recreational time so that it produces maximum relaxation for you and also affords opportunities to enrich your friendships with others, renew your creative energy, and give opportunities for Christian witness.

Seek the Lord's guidance, too, for the time you spend with your spouse and family. Ask Him to help you manage your family time so that relationships are made strong and joyful.

Key #3: Plan Your Schedule

Months can go by without your making any progress toward the fulfill-ment of your God-given goals if you don't plan your schedule and set your goals and dreams into the context of deadlines.

Organize your time for maximum productivity and efficiency. If morn-ings are your most productive hours, set aside those times for work directly related to your goals. Put your greatest concentration and effort into those hours. Don't allow appointments, phone calls, or meetings to drain the energy that you can better devote to productive work. Schedule appoint-ments, calls, and meetings for afternoon hours.

I heard about a man who does his best work when he is alone at the lab-oratory. He goes to work when most of the others at the lab are leaving, and then he works diligently until two o'clock in the morning. Those are his most productive hours in a day. He has learned to schedule his time, with his employer's blessing, so that he can get the maximum amount of quality work accomplished in any given day.

Most people I know find it easiest and most productive to spend time with the Lord first thing in the morning. They find that if they don't read their Bibles and spend time in prayer in the morning, they rarely get around to Bible reading and prayer during the rest of the day. Others find their best prayer and Bible-reading time is after all other family members have gone to bed. There is no set rule. Do what works for you!

Ask the Lord to show you how to set your schedule in any given day, week, and year to allow for a good balance of work and rest, alone time and family time, input and output.

Key #4: Stay Organized

Continually searching for missing documents or items is a waste of time. Stay organized as you work. Throughout the Bible, we find numer-ous references about doing things and maintaining things in an orderly fashion. (See Ex. 40:1–16 as an example.)

Recognize that your definition of being organized may be different from that of others. If you walk into my study, you are likely to find that most things are in their place, unless I'm right in the middle of studying something or writing a sermon. Then I usually have a stack of books open all around me and several pages of notes in various places. On the whole, however, I am a very orderly person.

Several staff members, however, are godly people who produce great work, but seem to work in the midst of chaos—at least from my perspective. Their offices have papers everywhere, stacks here, stacks there, even stacks on the floor. But if I ask one of them about a particular item or document, he can go directly to a stack, reach in about halfway down, and produce that item for me. There is organization—but only he knows it!

Organization is a key to efficiency. You can't get something done as quickly or smoothly without order and organization. Therefore, organization is important to maximizing your time.

Ask the Lord to help you remove the clutter from your life—the things that detract and pull you away from your God-given purpose and goals. Clutter includes time clutter—the things that clutter your schedule with unimportant activities and obligations.

Key #5: Rely on God's Wisdom

If you question the timing of anything in your life—when something should be done, how much time should be allotted to something, how often something should be done, the sequencing of a project—ask the Lord for His wisdom on the matter.

As you plan projects or break down large goals into specific tasks, ask the Lord, "Am I sequencing activities, events, or tasks in the right order? Am I allotting the appropriate amount of time for each facet of this project or task or event? Have I set the right deadlines?"

THE SUCCESSFUL USE OF TIME

Key #6: Eliminate the Unimportant

Charles Schwab, the president of Bethlehem Steel, hired a consultant and said to him, "If you'll show me how I and other top managers in our company can use our time better, I will pay you a fee of whatever you ask within reason."

The man said, "All right." He then gave Schwab a blank sheet of paper and said, "I want you to write on this sheet of paper all the important things you need to do tomorrow and list them in order of their priority. As number one, put the most important thing you should do tomorrow. As number two, put the second most important thing you should do, and so forth. Then when you go into work tomorrow morning, start with the first thing on your list and stick with it until you finish it. Then move on to number two, and so forth. You more than likely will not be able to accomplish all the things on your list in a given day, but you will have accomplished the most important thing on your list or at least made a major effort regarding it. Then tomorrow night, make a new list for the upcoming day. Do this for several weeks and let me know what happens."

The consultant concluded, "If you find that this plan is working for you, pass on the idea to your managers. And if this is of value to your company as a whole, send me a check for what you think the plan is worth."

Schwab did as the consultant advised, and he gave the idea to his managers, who also put the plan into action. A few weeks later, Schwab sent his consultant and friend, Ivy Lee, a check for twenty-five thousand dollars. In 1930, that amount was similar to receiving several hundred thousand dollars today. Schwab said to Ivy, "This is one of the most important ideas I have ever learned."

I am happy to pass along the idea to you. I have put this principle to work in my life, and I heartily recommend it. Every night, after looking at my schedule for the coming day, I write down on a three-by-five card the four most important things I hope to do the next day. I put the list in priority order, and one of the first things I do the next morning is look at that card. I carry the list with me to my work desk and keep it where I can see it readily. I have discovered that if I don't stay focused on what I truly want to get accomplished, phone calls and various interruptions can send me running in forty directions.

The things I write down are there because of their value to my broader purpose, which is to get the gospel to as many people as possible, as quickly as possible, as clearly as possible, as simply stated as possible, as irresistibly as possible, in the power of the Holy Spirit to the glory of God. Every day, I attempt to evaluate my schedule and my list of things to do in light of this question: Am I making progress toward my goal and toward the fulfillment of the main purpose for my life? If something doesn't fit into that broader purpose, it doesn't belong on my list of daily priorities.

I am absolutely convinced that if you will choose to lay aside all the things that result in a derailment or detour from God's main purpose for your life, you will be highly productive, more efficient, and in the end, very successful. We are wise to heed the same words the Lord said to Joshua about His plan for Joshua's life, "Do not turn from it to the right hand or to the left, that you may prosper wherever you go" (Josh. 1:7).

If someone or something interrupts your concentration, don't allow that person or thing to consume your entire day or derail you from your top priority for the day. If a crisis demands your immediate attention, don't allow that crisis to detour you from your God-given goals. Stay on track with your goals.

Of course, if you are under the authority of a supervisor or a "boss," from time to time you may be pulled away from what you perceive to be a priority in order to tackle an emergency situation or a "hot" item on the company agenda. In such situations, it may be wise to ask the person who is authorizing a new use of your time, "Is this a higher priority than the assignments you have already give me?" If the answer is yes, do the new assignment to the best of your ability. It has just become your number-one priority!

In the overall pattern of your life, doing a good job at the tasks put before you is part of God's plan for your life. Interruptions that are not frivolous or unavoidable may very well lead to a lesson that God has for you to learn, including the lesson of flexibility. All of us, however, know that many interruptions are simply time wasters, and they are the ones that nearly always can be avoided or cut short.

Key #7: Review Your Day

At the close of a day, review the way in which you have spent your time. Evaluate your schedule. Compare what you did with what you intended to do. Ask yourself:

- Did I make good use of my time?
- Did I procrastinate?
- Was I able to maintain my concentration?
- Did I engage in activities that truly were priorities?
- Did I make progress (even a little) toward the accomplishment of my God-given goals?

As you see yourself doing things you desire to do in order to be successful in God's eyes, give thanks and praise to God for His guidance, help, and encouragement.

If you recognize that you have made mistakes or have fallen short of the ideal schedule you set for yourself, ask the Lord's forgiveness for any sins you have committed in wasting time, and then ask for His help to do better the next day.

Don't give up on the pursuit of your goals! Make adjustments, learn from your mistakes, and begin the next day with fresh enthusiasm and courage.

As you put these seven principles into action on a daily, consistent basis, you are going to discover that you are not only growing in self-esteem, but also moving closer and closer to the fulfillment of God's purpose for your life. You will be *doing* what the Lord has set before you to do, and you will be in the process of *becoming* the person the Lord desires for you to be.

The wise use of time is the mark of discipline. And discipline is essential for success.

12

OVERCOMING THE NEGATIVES

What do you believe today about your success?

Do you believe success is possible?

Do you believe you are a success?

Do you believe that even greater success is possible for you tomorrow?

Negative responses to these questions can shut down success very quickly, and each of them is rooted in what a person believes.

In earlier chapters we discussed the relationship between attitudes and success, and thoughts and success. What you think is rooted in your mind. Thoughts are rational. They can be directed and focused and altered through the acquisition of new information, repetition, and a refocus of perspective.

Beliefs lie deeper in the soul. They are related to emotions and general attitude toward life. They are the source of your spontaneous responses to life. In many ways, they are much more pervasive and basic than your thoughts.

Beliefs are directly linked to motivation. They are the foundation for the way you view yourself, the world around you, and God.

To be successful, you must believe three things that are directly related to success:

1. "I *can* be a success."
2. "I am making progress toward success."
3. "God desires for me to be a success."

A failure to believe these three things strongly and consistently can be devastating to success.

Believe You Can Succeed

The apostle Paul wrote from a prison chamber in Rome, "I can do all things through Christ who strengthens me" (Phil. 4:13).

Is that what you believe today about yourself? Do you truly believe that you can accomplish what the Lord has helped you identify as goals for your life?

Paul did not say he could do all things in his own power. He said he could do all things *through Christ*. Paul drew his identity and his strength from Christ.

Moreover, Paul did not desire to do anything that was apart from Christ's purpose for him. He did not desire to fly without wings or pursue a career in an area where he was neither talented nor called by God. Paul sought to do only what Christ had called him to do and equipped him to do. Paul then said, with confidence, "I can do these things because Christ is fulfilling His purposes in me, and He is strengthening me in the very areas where He has equipped me. I can trust Christ to enable me to do what I desire to do and attempt to do, but am unable to do in my strength alone."

Every Christian can, and must, reach the point of making this same statement of affirmation—"I can do all things through Christ who strengthens me"—if he is truly to be successful. Why? Because the goals we set for ourselves are *God's* goals. Any goals that leave God out are not goals we can ever expect to achieve fully and with eternal benefit. If we set God's goals, then God is committed to helping us accomplish them. He promises to be with us, to provide for us, to empower us, and to give us courage to accomplish *His* goals for our lives.

With Christ, we cannot fail! We are always in the process of succeeding more and more.

As I have stated from the beginning, to be a genuine success is to seek continually to become the person God wants you to be and to pursue and achieve continuously the goals that God has set for you—God's person, God's goals, God's help! And with God's help, you cannot fail. You *will* succeed.

A person can be committed to a goal, enthusiastic about it, and work toward it with persistence, but if he doesn't truly believe he is going to succeed in accomplishing that goal, he will fall short. Something will be missing. And that missing something is going to cause that person to become less committed to the goal, less enthusiastic about the goal, and give less effort and be less persistent in pursuing the goal. The underlying motivation required for attaining a goal is going to fizzle.

Consider for a moment a student who enrolls in college intending to pursue a degree. He has a goal of earning a bachelor's degree in four years. He is enthusiastic about going to college. He starts attending college and doing his homework. But deep down inside, that student doesn't believe he is smart enough to finish college. He doesn't truly believe he can earn a college degree.

His belief about his ability to do college work may have many roots. Perhaps his parents, teachers, or friends have told him that he doesn't have what it takes for college. Perhaps he has had some negative experiences in high school, even failing a course or two. Perhaps he has doubts about where he will get the money to finish college. Whatever the root causes, he has a belief that he cannot earn a college degree. And that belief will counteract everything else over time unless he changes it.

His belief that he can't finish college will make him less committed to attending class, doing his assignments, or studying for tests. His belief will erode his enthusiasm for attending college, and he'll find more and more excuses to justify his poor performance in college and to pursue things other than college. In the end, the number-one reason he will fail to complete college is a lack of *believing*.

In contrast, consider the student who may not have great intellectual capacity or very good high school grades, but is accepted to a college and enrolls fully believing that she will graduate. She, too, has a goal and is enthusiastic about it. She, too, begins attending classes. As she studies and writes papers and takes exams, she does so with the firm conviction, "I can do this through Christ who strengthens me. God helped me to set this goal, and He is enabling me to accomplish it. *I am going to graduate*, with God's help."

Her belief in God keeps her burning the midnight oil as she studies. Her belief in God's help and calling keeps her at college, even if she makes less than top marks and even if she has to repeat a course. Her belief in God's help and calling sustains her motivation even if she has to work part-time as she studies and she takes six years instead of four to earn her degree. Her belief carries her across the finish line.

You can apply this same "I can do this, with Christ's help" belief to any pursuit in life—to being a spouse, parent, employee, salesman, pastor, singer, youth worker, missionary. If you believe you can do it, you very likely will do it. If you do not believe you can do it, you very likely won't.

The Bible never calls us to succeed apart from God's help. Our success always has a built-in faith element to it. Without faith, we aren't going to receive anything from God (James 1:6–8). Without faith, we do not access God's help.

Choose to be a person of faith today. Choose to believe that you can do all things that God has set before you to do because Christ will enable you to do them.

Believe God Is on Your Side

Another aspect of believing that is directly related to your success as a Christian is this: you must believe that God is on your side and that He is going to equip you, provide for you, empower you, and be present with you to do what He calls you to do.

Genuine success is rooted in the pursuit of the things that God has planned and purposed for your life. Your belief must remain strong that you are in pursuit of God's goals for you and that God desires for you to be successful in accomplishing the goals.

The writer of Hebrews declared, "He who comes to God must believe that He is, and that He is a rewarder of those who diligently seek Him" (11:6). What does this mean to you on a daily basis? It means that God is with you, and that He is working on your behalf to bring rewards to you as you seek and pursue His plan for you.

Many people who believe that God is *for* them fail to recognize that God is also *within* them to ensure that His beloved children succeed. Paul wrote, "He who calls you is faithful, who also will do it" (1 Thess. 5:24). The Lord who calls you to undertake a task also provides the power, wisdom, courage, and ability within you to see that task to full completion. God-given goals are just that: *God*-given goals. God is not going to help you set goals and then be uncommitted to and uninvolved in their attainment. The Holy Spirit has been imparted to you to give you a built-in divine ability to help you succeed.

Believe God's Principles Work

I recently encountered a person who said to me, "Oh, I believe God wants me to succeed. I'm just not sure *how* He wants me to succeed or to what degree He wants me to succeed." When in doubt, go to your Bible!

If you don't believe in the principles of the Bible, you won't act on them and apply them to your life. If you don't apply them, they won't work.

The opposite is equally true. If you believe in the principles of the Bible regarding a successful life, you will act on them and apply them. You will read God's Word, and you will do what it tells you to do. You will be eager to learn from God's Word and to apply what you learn. And as you apply God's principles, you will discover that the truth of the Bible works in your life.

Let me give you several examples. The conventional world wisdom is that a store must be open seven days a week. God's Word says,

> Six days you shall labor and do all your work, but the seventh day is the Sabbath of the LORD your God. In it you shall do no work: you, nor your son, nor your daughter, nor your male servant, nor your female servant, nor your cattle, nor your stranger who is within your gates. (Ex. 20:9–10)

Are you willing to obey what *God* says over what the world says? Do you truly *believe* this commandment of God?

The conventional world wisdom is that giving 10 percent of your earnings to the Lord is foolishness. God's Word says,

> Bring all the tithes into the storehouse,
> That there may be food in My house,
> And try Me now in this . . .
> If I will not open for you the windows of heaven
> And pour out for you such blessing
> That there will not be room enough to receive it. (Mal. 3:10)

The conventional world wisdom is that if you give anything away, you lose it. God's Word says, "Give, and it will be given to you: good measure, pressed down, shaken together, and running over will be put into your bosom" (Luke 6:38).

The conventional world wisdom is that to be successful, you must give as little as possible and take as much as possible. God's Word says, "With the same measure that you use [to give], it will be measured back to you" (Luke 6:38).

Which are you going to believe—the conventional wisdom of the world or God's Word? What you believe will determine what you do. And what you do will determine what God will do on your behalf.

Are you willing to believe what God's Word says about you? Are you willing to believe that God loves you, values you, and considers you worthy of success?

Are you willing to believe that God truly cares about your daily needs and desires to provide for you and help you through even the most difficult circumstances?

It isn't enough to believe that God exists and that His Word is true. You must believe that God exists *in* you by the power of His Holy Spirit and that His Word is true *for every aspect of your life.*

God Equips You for What He Requires of You

You must remind yourself often that whenever God requires something of you, God assumes the responsibility to enable you, equip you, and provide all the necessary resources for you to complete the job. If God has helped you set a goal, God will help you reach the goal. God never commands you to do anything He will not equip you to do. Neither will God ask you to do something and then fail to provide the necessary resources.

We see this principle borne out again and again in the Scriptures. Consider the example of Noah. God said to Noah,

> The end of all flesh has come before Me, for the earth is filled with violence through them; and behold, I will destroy them with the earth. Make yourself an ark of gopherwood; make rooms in the ark, and cover it inside and outside with pitch. (Gen. 6:13–14)

At the time God spoke to Noah, Noah had no concept of an ark. He had never seen one or heard about one or seen a picture of one. Furthermore, he had no idea *why* he should build an ark. He knew only that it had something to do with his protection and God's destruction of wicked mankind. God did not leave Noah in the dark about this, however. He said to him,

This is how you shall make it: The length of the ark shall be three hundred cubits, its width fifty cubits, and its height thirty cubits. You shall make a window for the ark, and you shall finish it to a cubit from above; and set the door of the ark in its side. You shall make it with lower, second, and third decks. (Gen. 6:15–16)

God revealed *how* Noah was to build an ark.

Then God revealed *why* Noah was to build the ark:

I Myself am bringing floodwaters on the earth, to destroy from under heaven all flesh in which is the breath of life; everything that is on the earth shall die. But I will establish My covenant with you; and you shall go into the ark—you, your sons, your wife, and your sons' wives with you. And of every living thing of all flesh you shall bring two of every sort into the ark, to keep them alive with you; they shall be male and female. Of the birds after their kind, of animals after their kind, and of every creeping thing of the earth after its kind, two of every kind will come to you to keep them alive. And you shall take for yourself of all food that is eaten, and you shall gather it to yourself; and it shall be food for you and for them. (Gen. 6:17–21)

God explained what He was going to do, what Noah was to do, and how God intended for events to unfold. Noah was given clear direction about *how* to respond to God's command. He was equipped with knowledge. Notice, too, that the Lord said, "Two of every kind will come to you to keep them alive." Noah didn't have to go out and seek all of the species that were to be kept alive in the ark. God was going to cause them to go to Noah, and Noah was to take care of them.

We read in Genesis 6:22, "Thus Noah did; according to all that God commanded him, so he did."

It took Noah more than one hundred years to complete the ark and for all of the animals to be gathered. And throughout those years, God provided. He gave Noah the strength and materials and know-how to gather the gopherwood, build the ark, and cover it with pitch. He gave Noah three sons, and each was married by the time the "fountains of the great deep were broken up, and the windows of heaven were opened" (Gen. 7:11). Noah was given the provision and help necessary to get the job done.

If God calls you to do something—even to a goal you don't understand fully—you can trust God to provide for you the knowledge you need, the provision you need, and the help you need. He calls you not to fail, but to succeed. He will provide for you everything you need to get the job done successfully.

When the Lord called Moses to return to Pharaoh with the message, "Let My people go," Moses argued that the people would not listen to him or believe that the Lord had sent him with the message. What did God do? He provided a means of proof to the people that He had sent Moses: a rod that became a serpent when it was cast on the ground, and regained its shape as a rod when Moses took hold of it. He also told Moses to put his hand in his bosom and draw it out—and when Moses did so, his hand was leprous. Then the Lord told Moses to put his hand again in his bosom, and when he drew it out again, his hand was restored like his other flesh. The Lord said, "And if they don't believe these two signs, take water from the river and pour it on the dry land, and it will become blood" (Ex. 4:1–9).

Moses argued further that he was ill-equipped for the task since he was not an eloquent speaker but was "slow of speech and slow of tongue" (Ex. 4:10). The Lord said, "I will be with your mouth and teach you what you shall say," and He also gave Moses the assurance that his brother, Aaron, would be by his side to act as his spokesman since the Lord would be with his mouth as well (Ex. 4:11–16).

What excuses are you using today for not pursuing the goals you believe God has set before you? God's word to you is that He will provide the skills and abilities necessary, and He will cause you to be effective in your relating to other people.

Don't let others tell you what you can and cannot do in your pursuit of God's goals. Trust God to provide what you need in order to accomplish what He calls you to do. He will reveal to you precisely what you need and what tactics you are to employ.

Ask God for His guidance every step of the way. The apostle Paul certainly did. Paul was totally reliant on the Holy Spirit to show him where he was to go, to whom he was to speak, with whom he was to stay, what he was to do, how long he was to stay, when he was to leave, and where he was to go next. At times, he made his plans to the best of his ability only to have the Holy Spirit reveal to him, "Go here instead." And Paul was faithful to the leading of the Lord each time.

We have no mention in the Scriptures that Paul consciously planned to preach in the major cities of the Roman Empire where transportation and communication systems were developed to the greatest extent so that thousands of people might not only hear the gospel but also take it to the far reaches of the earth. But as Paul followed the leading of the Holy Spirit, that is precisely what happened. He had remarkable results in places such as Corinth and Ephesus—large cities that were major ports, key cities on major trade routes, and centers of international commerce. Paul had a goal of preaching the gospel to as many people as possible, as effectively as possible. The Holy Spirit filled in the details about where and how and to whom.

Trust God to do for you what He did for Noah, Moses, and Paul. Trust the Holy Spirit for the practical how-to's related to your success. Believe that God will equip you fully for all He has called you to do.

An Ongoing Revelation

In 1989 I was in a hotel room in Kansas City, walking toward the window to look out, when the Lord spoke in my heart, "I am going to make your name a household word around the world." I stepped back and thought to myself, *Stanley, that's the most egotistical thought you've ever had.* And then I thought again, *But I didn't think that up. I've never had any desire for my name to be a household word around the world.* I said, "Lord, if that's of You, how could that possibly be?"

Immediately my attention was directed to the top of a building across the way from the hotel. It was covered with satellite dishes and antennas. I didn't understand fully how the Lord was going to do what He had spoken in my heart, but I knew it had something to do with media. I never spoke a word of this to anyone in those days—in fact, not until just a few months ago.

In 1991, two years later, I was on a retreat with my staff members. We had spent part of the morning reading the Bible, praying, and taking walks to listen to what God might say to us individually. When we met together as a group, I felt led to turn to the last words of Jesus recorded in the gospel of Matthew: "Go into all the world and make disciples of all nations." I stopped reading and asked one of my associates, "Is it possible to get the gospel into all nations?" He said, "Yes, I believe it is."

We prayed some more and talked about how we might get the gospel into every nation.

I said, "Let's set our minds and energies toward doing this within two years, but not tell anybody about it. Let's see what God will do." And we began to plan and work. One week short of two years later, we were on the air with the gospel—by means of television, radio, or shortwave radio—into every nation of the earth.

I didn't make the connection between 1989 in Kansas City and 1991 on retreat until recently. And then it became clear—God knew all along what He wanted to do and was going to do. But for me, a worldwide media ministry has been an unfolding revelation.

God may not tell you all you need to know at the outset of your pursuing a goal. He may have goals, methods, and means that unfold before you as you take each step of faith. Look for God's continuing revelation to you.

Turning Belief into Reality

The process of belief is actually a very simple one. The stronger you believe something, the more you are motivated to act on that belief. The steps from belief to action are these:

Visualize Your Success

Your belief will trigger your imagination. You will be able to visualize yourself doing what you believe God is calling you to do.

Do you believe God has called you and equipped you to be an outstanding salesman, one who uses his earnings to help fund the spreading of the gospel around the world? If you truly believe that, you are going to be able to see yourself making sales. You are going to be able to visualize yourself closing deals and seeing people sign up for what you are offering or purchase what you are selling. You are also going to be able to visualize giving your earnings to a project that the Lord has revealed to you as one worthy of your gifts. You are going to be able to see that ministry impacting lives for Christ—winning souls, encouraging believers, and teaching others the truth of God's love and the commandments of God's Word.

Have you lost your job? Do you believe that God has another job for you, one that is even better suited to your abilities? Are you able to visualize yourself going to an interview and being confident in that interview and landing that job? Are you able to visualize yourself doing excellent work in your new job? Are you able to visualize yourself working with others in that place of employment, creating and developing and producing new products and projects that are of benefit to the world?

Your ability to visualize your success is directly related to your belief. It flows from your belief, and in turn, it strengthens your belief.

The Bible tells us, "Faith is the substance of things hoped for, the evidence of things not seen" (Heb. 11:1). There is nothing wrong with visualizing godly success. That is the very essence of faith, which is believing for God's plan and purpose to be fulfilled.

Being able to visualize your success reinforces your confidence. Have you ever been asked to give a talk to a group of people, but you were petrified at the thought? Check your believing. Do you really believe God can help you do this? The stronger your belief that, in Christ, you can give this talk and that God wants you to give the talk, the greater your motivation will be to prepare a good talk and to deliver it with confidence. Visualize yourself giving a successful talk. Visualize yourself standing behind the lectern, smiling confidently at the audience before you, and delivering the message God has enabled you to prepare.

Do you believe God can help you overcome a particular type of temptation? Visualize yourself in a tempting situation and walking away from that temptation.

Do you believe God can help you overcome a bad habit? Visualize yourself saying no to an impulse to engage in that habit.

Visualize what you want to be, want to do, and want to accomplish. Visualize how you want to live and how you want to work, relate to others, and pursue goals.

Don't visualize negatives. Visualize the positives that God has set before you as commandments, goals, and godly desires.

Drive Away the Cobwebs of Disbelief About Your Success

Cobwebs can appear in even the cleanest homes. The same is true for the cobwebs of doubt that can invade your believing. There is no sin in having doubts; the real issue is what you choose to do when you have doubts.

As you visualize your success in any area of life, doubt is likely to erupt—suddenly, unexpectedly, and perhaps enormously. You'll find yourself doubting if you have heard God, wondering if God is really with you, feeling inferior and unworthy, comparing yourself to others. The negatives may seem endless.

Immediately you must take authority over that doubt. Just as you would say about a cobweb hanging in your dining room, "I can get rid of that with just one swipe of the broom," you must say to a cobweb of doubt, "I can banish this with a swipe of faith." And then get out the broom of your faith and go to work! Proclaim the promises of God. Quote or read aloud Scripture to yourself. Focus on verses that speak of God's power, authority, ability, and desire to impart to you His presence.

The more you confront a doubt with expressions of faith, the more readily your doubt is going to vanish, and with it, fear is going to dissipate.

As a part of confronting doubt, choose to speak positive words of faith *aloud*. They can be verses of Scripture. They can also be positive statements about yourself or the situation at hand.

Consider for a moment a cook who prepares a meal and then says to her guests before the meal begins, "This may not be fit to eat, but let's gather around the table anyway," or "I've got a new oven, so I'm not sure if this dish is really cooked sufficiently, but let's try it." What is your reaction going to be as a guest? You are probably going to be reluctant to eat.

But another cook may say to her guests, "This is one of my favorite recipes," or "I could hardly wait to taste this dish from the time I first read the recipe." What is your reaction going to be? You likely are going to be salivating even before you sit down at the table!

If we do not come to grips with our doubts, and do so quickly, our doubts can escalate into paralyzing fear. As we read in the book of Job:

> For the thing I greatly feared has come upon me,
> And what I dreaded has happened to me.

I am not at ease, nor am I quiet;
I have no rest, for trouble comes. (Job 3:25–26)

When doubt and fear rise up in you, you must forget about past failures, turn a deaf ear to the criticisms of others, and move forward with your faith. Get your eyes off your doubts and fears and onto the Lord.

Speak what you know to be true from *God's* perspective. Choose to trust that His Word is true and that He will equip you to visualize the very success He is calling you to experience. Keep in mind always that what you say to dispel your doubts and fears does a great deal to impact what you will eventually do.

Take a Bold Action Step

The stronger your belief and the greater your ability to wipe away the cobwebs of doubt, the more likely you will be to take a bold step toward your goal. Do something positive toward accomplishing the goal that God has helped you set. Don't wait until you can take a huge step. Take the step you are able to take right now. You'll be one step closer to success.

Ten Tips to Strengthen Your Belief System

A strong belief system is essential as you begin to take steps toward your goal and all along the pathway to success. Here are ten ways to strengthen your belief system that you can apply to any situation and build into any day:

1. *State with confidence and boldness: "God has endowed me with everything I need to be what He wants me to be and to accomplish what He wants me to accomplish."* Remind yourself of this truth repeatedly, as often as necessary.

2. *Remind yourself often of the Lord's promise to make a way when there seems to be no way.* Reread portions of Scripture that illustrate this truth— Daniel's release from the lions' den, the deliverance of Shadrach, Meshach, and Abed-Nego from a fiery furnace, the opening of the Red Sea so the

Israelites might cross it, the provision made for Elijah as he ran for his life from Jezebel, Peter's release from Herod's prison, the provision of the wise men for the flight of Joseph, Mary, and the young child Jesus to Egypt, the resurrection of Jesus from the dead. No matter how dark or disappointing things may seem to be, choose to recall: God can make a way!

3. *Highlight every verse in your Bible that deals with courage, confidence, faith, and believing.* I suggest using a colored pencil so that you can lightly shade these verses. You will find as you thumb through your Bible that it is filled from cover to cover with verses that build faith. You'll also find that these verses are easy to access just when you most need a boost to your faith.

4. *Pray the promises of God.* As you read aloud verses of promise, turn them into prayers, saying, "Lord, You have said in Your word . . ." The Lord doesn't need a reminder, but *you do*! In reminding God of His promises, you are reinforcing the truth of these promises to yourself.

5. *Visualize and affirm your assets.* Remind yourself of your talents, skills, abilities, and good qualities of character. Visualize yourself using your assets to maximum productivity with maximum quality. See yourself establishing good relationships and doing excellent work, with a smile on your face and joy in your heart. Don't just say, "I'm *trying* to do my best." Instead, say, "I'm becoming the best I can possibly be!"

Any person who focuses only on his faults and failures is going to end up in depression. Choose to focus on the good traits and talents God has built into your life.

6. *Make a list of character qualities you want to develop and then memorize your list.* Turn your attention from what you are doing and what you want to do, to what kind of person you are and desire to become. Make a list of the character traits that you desire to be known for, and then ask the Lord to help you develop those traits. Visualize yourself speaking, responding, and acting as a spiritually mature person would speak, respond, and act.

7. *Actively replace negative thoughts and statements with positive thoughts and statements.* Monitor continually your thought life and speech. When

you catch yourself thinking or speaking negatively, immediately think a positive thought or speak a positive word. Make an active, concerted, intentional effort to replace your negative speech and thought patterns. Consider words such as *can't, won't,* and *couldn't* to be red flags in your thinking and speaking. Reemphasize to yourself, "I *can* do all things through Christ who strengthens me!"

8. *When an obstacle arises, state boldly, "If God is for me, who can be against me?" (Rom. 8:31).* Is God big enough, great enough, powerful enough, wise enough, and strong enough to handle any problem you can imagine? Absolutely! Paul also wrote of our Lord that He is "able to do exceedingly abundantly above all that we ask or think" (Eph. 3:20).

When you are incapable, He is able. When you are weak, He is strong. When you don't know, He *does* know. When you are powerless, He is all-powerful. When you don't have an answer, He does. The Lord is capable of handling any problem, any enemy, any obstacle, anytime, and anywhere.

9. *When you are feeling harassed by Satan, say aloud, "Father God, I want to thank You that You are greater in me than anything Satan can do to me."* Remind yourself of 1 John 4:4: "He who is in you is greater than he who is in the world."

10. *Remind yourself continually, "God is with me in this."* God is not confused, troubled, fearful, doubtful, or weary—at any time or about anything. God is with you always. He will never leave you or forsake you. He is ever-present to help you in all things that are in line with His commandments and His highest plans and purposes for your life.

Expect to Succeed

Go into any new project, task, or opportunity with the idea, "Let me see what I can do!" Rather than focus on problems or obstacles that *might* arise, set a goal that you believe is possible to accomplish. And expect to succeed at reaching that goal.

A friend said to me, "I had about twenty hours of work to do the last day before I had to leave on an international business trip. I had no idea how I was going to get everything done, but when I went to bed the night before, I prayed, 'Lord, give me a good night's rest so I'll have the energy I need to give it my best tomorrow.'

"When I awoke that morning at six o'clock, I prayed for the Lord's wisdom and energy, and I also prayed that I'd have no wasted motion and no unnecessary interruptions in the day ahead. I concentrated my focus on the tasks at hand and dived in. To my great surprise, I had everything done by ten o'clock that night. I even had a chance to rerun some of the numbers in my report to double-check their accuracy. I was packed and ready for the trip!"

Another person once said to me, "When I don't know if I can get something done in the time designated, I say, 'Well, I don't know that I *can't* get it done,' so I start in and give it my all. I usually get it done!"

Choose to Believe

Are you aware that your body cannot distinguish between what is real and what is imagined? If a giant grizzly bear weighing about two thousand pounds lumbered into the room where you are reading right now, you'd no doubt jump up and run for your life. And rightly so! But what if a person came into the shadows of your tent out in the wilderness in a very realistic grizzly bear outfit, making very realistic grizzly bear sounds? You'd still run! Why? Because your mind isn't going to take any chances about whether or not that image is real. It is going to react to what it perceives—a big furry object that looks and sounds and moves like a vicious grizzly bear!

When you imagine yourself succeeding, your body and mind move in the direction of that success. A mental pathway is created that is just as real over time as if you really *were* doing what you are imagining yourself doing. Your body lines up its spontaneous reactions so that a built-in propensity to act in a positive, successful way is created.

The same is true, however, if you imagine failure. You are setting up mental pathways and propensities to fail.

A man once had an idea that he thought would help people, and he wrote a book explaining it. He sent the manuscript to a number of publishers, and each one rejected it. He finally said, "I've failed. I'm going to forget this project and move on." He tossed the manuscript in the trash can of his office, and when his wife reached in to pull it out, he said, "Don't take that out of the trash can." She didn't. But the next day as she was emptying the trash, she had an idea.

She went personally to a publisher her husband hadn't contacted, and she said, "I have a manuscript I'd like for you to consider." She reached down and lifted a large object from the floor next to her and placed it on his desk. It was wrapped in brown paper, much larger than any book manuscript he had ever seen. He said, "Well, what kind of manuscript is it?" She said, "Open it and you'll see." When the publisher unwrapped it, he found a trash can, and in the trash can, the manuscript of the woman's husband. She hadn't removed it from the trash, but she also hadn't emptied it *from* the trash. He was so intrigued with what had happened that he went home and read the manuscript from first page to last. He liked what he read, and he published the book. It became a number-one seller around the world.

Is it possible to keep from getting discouraged or having doubts about your ability to succeed or your work? No.

Is it possible to keep from questioning occasionally whether you are on the right track or whether God is with you? No.

Is it possible to keep from wondering if certain principles in God's Word will work? No.

But it is possible in these moments of doubt to choose to believe. It is possible to reaffirm that God has called you to success, God is with you, and His Word is true. It is possible to encourage yourself with the Word of God and to build up your faith and strengthen your power to believe.

You can become the person God has ordained you to be.

You can achieve every goal God has set for you.

You can always count on God's Word as truth.

You can rely on God to be with you and to help you.

Believe it!

13

Persisting Until You Succeed

⁓

I have never met a person who didn't want to succeed at *something*. At the same time, I have met very few people who succeed at *everything*—or even most things—they believe to be God-given goals for their lives.

Many people who desire to succeed start out right, and they reach a moderate level of success. But then at the first obstacle they hit, they allow discouragement to set in. If they do nothing to counteract discouragement and to remedy the situation or resolve the problem, both the obstacle and the discouragement remain. Over time, they give up and settle for the level of success they had achieved at the time they first encountered problems and became discouraged. That level of success is far less than what they might have achieved.

God has an *ever-growing plan and purpose* for you. You will never fully arrive at all you can be; you will never do all that you are capable of doing. But each day you are called to continue to become what God sets out as the character pattern for you: the fullness of the maturity of Christ Jesus. And you are called to continue to pursue the goals that God has helped you set for your life. There are no justifications in God's Word for remaining discouraged or for giving up.

Just as God does not give you a child for you to abandon that child, so God does not give you a goal for you to abandon it far short of achieving it. You are called to persist, to persevere, to endure. Until when? Until the *end*, which is the day you die or Jesus returns to this earth!

The One Trait of All Successful People

Persistence is the one trait that you are going to find in the life of every person who has achieved something worthwhile. It is the trait of a successful mother or father, businessman, factory worker, pastor, builder, artist, musician, teacher, or doctor. You name the profession or area of service and ministry, and you'll find persistence as a character trait for those who are at the top of that field.

Persistence is the combination of strong desire and willpower. It is the capacity to continue on course despite all manner of difficulties, obstacles, and discouragement—and not quit. When others say, "I'm not sure if it's going to work," or "It's looking impossible," those who are persistent say, "Let's try even harder. Let's continue on." Persistence is raw determination to move forward rather than to stop or slide backward.

When everybody else gives up on your child, persist in your love and efforts on behalf of that child.

When everyone gives up on you in your sickness or trouble, persist in your faith and efforts to overcome and be made whole.

When all others see no future, continue to believe God for a bright tomorrow.

That's being *persistent*.

To the Corinthians, Paul wrote of various trials and difficult circumstances he had undergone in his walk with the Lord:

Are they ministers of Christ? . . . I am more: in labors more abundant, in stripes above measure, in prisons more frequently, in deaths often. From the Jews five times I received forty stripes minus one. Three times I was beaten with rods; once I was stoned; three times I was shipwrecked; a night and a day I have been in the deep; in journeys often, in perils of waters, in perils of robbers, in perils of my own countrymen, in perils of the Gentiles, in perils in the city, in perils in the wilderness, in perils in the sea, in perils among false brethren; in weariness and toil, in sleeplessness often, in hunger and thirst, in fastings often, in cold and nakedness—besides the other things, what comes upon me daily: my deep concern for all the churches. (2 Cor. 11:23–28)

Is there any person alive today who has gone through so much hardship, pain, and difficulty in the pursuit of his goal? And yet, there is no indication that Paul ever gave up or decided that his current level of maturity in Christ Jesus was sufficient.

The vast majority of Christians I know would have experienced about one-tenth of what Paul experienced and then concluded, "God must not have called me to this. If He had, it would be easier." The fact is, God never calls us to an easy life. He calls us to persevere regardless of outer circumstances in our pursuit of what He has helped us to set as God-given goals.

The Determining Factor of Persistence

What determines how persistent we are?

The value we place on a goal.

If our goals are unfocused and uncertain, we aren't going to be very persistent in our pursuit of them. If our goals are set too low, we'll feel no need to be persistent. If our goals are of our own making, we'll feel no abiding commitment to them, and therefore, we will not be persistent in pursuing them. But if our goals are well defined, from God, and present a major challenge to us, we will value them highly, and we will pursue them diligently.

How important are your goals to you today?

Are they a matter of life and death—if not for you, perhaps for someone else?

Do your goals involve eternal life and death for others?

If your goals do not have high value or great purpose, I encourage you to reevaluate your goals. God may desire for you to do far more.

If a mother sees her beloved baby snatched from his crib, she is going to chase the abductors until she has her baby back. Even if she falls by the roadside in exhaustion, she is going to get up and continue her pursuit until she holds her baby in her arms again. There will be no stopping her, no fruitless end to her search. That's the same way you are to pursue your goals.

Jesus offered several parables in which persistence was a key factor. In the gospel of Luke, we read these words of Jesus:

> What man of you, having a hundred sheep, if he loses one of them, does not leave the ninety-nine in the wilderness, and go after the one which is lost until he finds it? And when he has found it, he lays it on his shoulders, rejoicing . . . Or what woman, having ten silver coins, if she loses one coin, does not light a lamp, sweep the house, and search carefully until she finds it? . . . Likewise, I say to you, there is joy in the presence of the angels of God over one sinner who repents. (Luke 15:4–10)

"But," you may say, "you don't know my circumstances." No, I don't. But I can tell you this, no matter what difficulty or hardship you are going through, someone else has already gone through that hardship and persisted in seeking a solution or in enduring that hardship until he came out on the side of victory. The more biographies of people you read, both long and short, of both famous and unknown people, the more you are going to discover that there isn't a problem known to man that hasn't been faced and *overcome* by a persistent person.

The apostle Paul had three significant things going for him in his pursuit of his goal, which was to evangelize the Mediterranean world.

First, Paul knew that God had given him his goals. There was no denial of his Damascus Road experience. Paul knew that Jesus had saved him and given him the commission to spread the gospel. Are you certain today that God has given you your goals? If not, you need to spend time with the Lord until you are certain that the goals you are pursuing are *His* goals for your life.

Second, Paul had a very clear goal—to get the gospel not only to Jews but also to Gentiles. Can you state your goals in a clear, concise way? Are there any fuzzy areas or questionable aspects of your goals? If so, ask the Lord for clarification.

Third, Paul felt indebted to get the truth to those who were without the truth. He felt responsible for pursuing his goal of preaching the gospel because he knew the difference the gospel could make in people's lives. He felt responsible for fulfilling the plan and purpose of God for his life because he valued highly his salvation.

How thankful are you today for your salvation? How thankful are you for the life of Christ that you lead? Do you feel responsible for sharing the life of Christ with others? If not, ask the Lord to reveal to you the full price and the full value of your salvation. Ask Him to reveal to you what the future holds for those who do not know Christ Jesus as their Savior. Paul had a clear conviction about the eternal destruction of judgment that awaits those who die without Christ. He wrote to the Corinthians, "The love of Christ compels us" (2 Cor. 5:14).

If you truly know that your goals are from God, that they are clear and certain, and that they are related to the eternal life or death of lost souls, you are going to place very high value on your goals. How can you not persist in pursuing them? Nothing could stop the apostle Paul from pressing on, and nothing will be able to stop you if your goals have these three characteristics.

Jesus certainly had these three qualities related to His goal, which was to lay down His life at Calvary to atone for your sin and mine. He said repeatedly that was the purpose for which He had been predestined from before the foundation of the world. In His life on this earth, Jesus gave us a beautiful pattern by which to live. But the real purpose of His life was to be found in His death.

In Luke 9:51 we read this about Jesus as He approached the culmination of His reason for being on the earth: "Now it came to pass, when the time had come for Him to be received up, that He steadfastly set His face to go to Jerusalem." There was an absolute, stone-faced, unreserved determination of Jesus to go to Jerusalem and to the cross. Nothing could have stopped Him. He had come into the world for this reason.

As Jesus made that journey, He said to several of those who walked with Him, "Follow Me." One man replied, "Lord, let me first go and bury my father." Another said, "Lord, I will follow You, but let me first go and bid them farewell who are at my house." Jesus said to them, "No one, having put his hand to the plow, and looking back, is fit for the kingdom of God" (Luke 9:59–62).

It takes persistence to live out a godly life on this earth, to proclaim Christ no matter what others say, and to endure and *grow* in an intimate relationship with the Lord. There is no giving up. Your commitment must be total and unwavering.

There is no going to church for a few years and then quitting.

There is no praying for a few minutes a day for a few months and then stopping.

There is no reading a few books of the Bible and then calling it quits.

No! The life you are to live in Christ Jesus is a life you are to pursue with a "press on" attitude until the moment you die. It's a lifelong walk of faith, regardless of circumstances. It's a persistent call to mature into the full stature of the likeness of Christ Jesus.

What About Retirement?

The world tells you to retire at age sixty-five or seventy. The world even values those who have been able to earn enough money to take early retirement. God's Word says there is no retirement for the believer. The goals God gives to you are lifelong goals. You must never stop growing, stop witnessing, stop praying, stop studying God's Word, stop learning, stop attending church, or stop doing what you can to help others.

What About Striving?

There are those who claim that you are to cease all striving and to "rest" in the Lord (Ps. 46:10; 37:7). Do these admonitions mean you are not to persist or to press on with diligence and steadfastness? No. These verses about resting in the Lord are related to putting your trust in the Lord. You are to rest in Him completely, ceasing from all self-striving, and trust Him with your whole heart. The finest examples of ceasing from self-striving and of placing complete trust in the Lord are to be found in a persistent pursuit of Christ.

A pursuit of godly goals is rooted in Christ's strength, Christ's purposes, Christ's wisdom. The person who persists in pursuing a mature life in Christ is no longer striving to make things happen on his own strength, power, and ability, but is trusting the Lord completely to do His work in and through his life.

Did Jesus struggle and strive to make things happen? No. He trusted the Father. Even in Gethsemane when His soul was torn apart in agony and grief, He trusted the Father.

Why Is Persistence So Important?

Persistence is required if you are going to overcome discouragement. Persistence is vital to success because defeats, failures, mistakes, and delays are inevitable.

It doesn't make any difference how highly you develop your skills or how knowledgeable you become in a particular field, you are going to make mistakes and experience periods of failure from time to time. We live in a fallen world, and there is no getting away from the inevitability of error. The problem with failures, faults, and mistakes is that many of us don't know how to deal with them. We allow ourselves to become discouraged by them, even if we know we are learning valuable lessons by experiencing them.

In his time, Christopher Columbus was dismissed as a fool by most people. But he pursued his goal until he reached it.

Thomas Edison was one of the most notable inventors in American history. Did you know he had less than three months of formal schooling? Did you know that by his own estimation, he conducted ten thousand experiments that failed? Nevertheless, he pursued his goals until he reached them.

Babe Ruth was one of the greatest home-run hitters of all time. Did you know he also holds the record for the most strikeouts? Every time Babe Ruth went to the plate to bat, however, he had only one thought: hit the ball over the fence. He didn't give up.

Persistence is required if you are going to succeed in your witness for Christ.

For three summers while I was in college, I worked at a textile mill. I was assigned to the bleachery—an extremely hot and uncomfortable area where the fabric went through vats of bleach. The men who worked fulltime in that area were pretty rough. I don't know where they picked up the term since I was only eighteen years old when I began working in that mill, but the men began to call me "the deacon."

At first, I was called the deacon with a tone of ridicule. The other guys made fun of my references to the Lord and my desire to talk about God. But about three weeks into my first summer of work, I noticed a change in my coworkers. They didn't criticize me as much. When I came around, their dirty jokes and profanity stopped. A few even apologized for the way they had treated me the first few days on the job.

The next summer when I returned to the mill, most of those men were still there. They were happy to see me. They treated me right. I didn't hear any dirty language or dirty jokes. God was doing something in their lives.

And by the third summer, some of the men started asking me to tell them what I believed and why. I had an opportunity to witness to them. A couple of those men began to attend church with their wives.

I could have kept my mouth shut the entire three summers I worked at that mill, and it probably would have been exactly the same place on the day I left it as it was the day I arrived. But that isn't God's plan for any of us. He expects us to be transformed and then to transform the environments in which we find ourselves. We do that by persisting in our pursuit of God's goals for our lives—both in what we are to *be* and in what we are to *do*.

What goals are you pursuing today? Are you refusing to give up? Are you *persisting*?

Five Principles to Learn About Persistence

You must learn five key principles if you want to strengthen your resolve to persist until you reach your goals:

1. A person is not a failure just because he fails. "Being a failure" and "having a failure" are two different things. Every successful person has a number of failures. The difference is, the successful person keeps getting up each time he is knocked down. You aren't a failure until you give up.

2. A test does not mean that you are to stop pursuing a goal. A test does not mean "stop here." A test is an opportunity to learn a valuable lesson on your way to reaching your goals. A temporary setback should be just that—temporary. You may experience a delay or face a problem to overcome, but don't regard that obstacle as a permanent and insurmountable roadblock. Find a way to go over, under, around, or tunnel through that obstacle!

3. In every failure, you'll find a seed of equivalent success. Choose to learn something from every mistake. Every time you experience a failure or make a mistake, choose to count it as a lesson in what not to do. When you know what *not* to do, what *to do* becomes clearer.

4. Bury your failures. Don't frame your failures or keep revisiting them with remorse. Bury them and move on. If forgiveness is required, ask God to forgive you, and ask others to forgive you. But then forgive yourself, and get busy again in the pursuit of your God-given goals. The only reason to remember a failure or a sin is to avoid doing it again. Choose to learn the lesson from your mistake, and press on toward what lies ahead of you that is positive.

Some people become so committed to telling their testimony about how God saved them that they never press on and develop an even greater testimony about how God has helped them to grow, develop, and mature. Press on. Keep your testimony updated daily. Your testimony shouldn't be limited to what God did for you twenty years ago. It should include what God did twenty months ago, twenty weeks ago, twenty days ago, and what He is doing right now.

5. Be quick to forgive others. You can get so caught up in the blame game that you lose all momentum in the pursuit of your goals. You can blame others and refuse to forgive others who hurt you all you like, but the truth remains:

- You are responsible for your actions, responses, and feelings.
- There is never any justification in hurting someone else, harboring unforgiveness, or taking vengeance into your own hands.
- You have a choice rooted in your free will about what you choose to do in the face of persecution, injury, criticism, or hurt feelings.
- The blame game always hurts you more than it hurts others. The blame game stunts your spiritual growth, damages your fellowship with God, and promotes disharmony with others.

When you continually blame others, you actually choose to live in a state of unforgiveness. You hold others responsible for your pain, and you refuse to forgive them for what they have done to you. As long as you refuse to forgive, you cannot be forgiven (Luke 6:37). Jesus was very clear on this point. You must forgive others if you are to receive God's forgiveness.

Many years ago, a man I know loaned a friend twelve thousand dollars, which was a significant amount to him at that time and represented virtually all of his savings. His friend mismanaged the money and lost it all. Not only that, but he began to bad-mouth the friend who had loaned him the money and disassociated himself completely from their friendship. The man faced a question, How should he respond to the borrower?

He talked it over with another friend one day, and the friend said, "Well, you know you're going to have to forgive him." The man said, "Forgive him? After what he did?" But the seed of God's truth had been planted. The more the man prayed about that situation and read God's Word, the more he knew he had to forgive the man and go on.

He forgave that man in a specific prayer and intentional prayer of forgiveness. It was a day of tremendous freedom and victory for him. And what did the Lord do? Within a year, the Lord had restored every penny that man had loaned. Not only did he experience financial restoration, but he had joy and peace in his heart that he had done the right thing before God.

He was able to move forward, without any hindrance in his faith or in his pursuit of his goals. What could have been a major disappointment or stumbling block to him had been removed.

As long as you live in a state of unforgiveness toward those who wrong you, the Lord cannot bless you and cause your efforts to prosper. I'm not referring to being born again here: I'm referring to refusing to forgive the sins of those who hurt, injure, reject, or criticize you. Choose to forgive! You will release yourself to move forward toward God's goals for your life.

Developing a Spirit of Persistence

In addition to learning the five principles noted, you can do several things to develop a spirit of persistence:

Set Goals That Demand Your Best

Don't settle for second-best goals that can be achieved with a less-than-excellent effort. Set high goals that require excellence in character, skill, and effort. Remember always that you are pursuing a God of excellence.

Develop a Burning Desire to See Your Goal Become a Reality

Deepen your commitment toward your goal. Study and work at your goal until you have a passion to accomplish it. Paul didn't say to himself, "Well, if the opportunity ever arises, I'd like to travel to Ephesus, and if it's convenient, I'd like to share the gospel with some people while I'm there." No! He had a burning desire in his soul to reach the lost in as many places as possible.

If you have allowed people to throw cold water on the flame that was once burning in your soul and spirit, ask God to reignite your heart and to cause His goals for you to begin to burn within you. Get excited about your goals!

Keep Your Eyes on the Goal

Don't be led astray by every new offer or better deal. Someone will always present to you an appealing side track or detour. Stay focused on the goals that God has set before you.

Refuse to Listen to Negative Criticism

No matter who is criticizing you or your efforts, refuse to pay attention to negative comments. Advice is another matter. Good advice, rooted in a desire to see you succeed and to do so with as few errors as possible, is highly valuable. But don't heed criticism—a tearing down of your idea; an effort to diminish the value of your goal; an effort to thwart a good cause, service, or production of a good product; a criticism of the Lord and of ministries that serve Him; or criticism aimed at your personal character, appearance, or physical traits. Listen to what God says about you.

Surround Yourself with People Who Will Encourage You

You'll find it much easier to persist in the pursuit of your goals if you are surrounded by people who encourage you onward and who believe, as you do, that God is with you and God will help you. Work with those who desire to help you, pray for you, and believe that what you are doing is valuable in God's eyes.

Don't listen to idle flattery, which is usually offered in an attempt to manipulate or control you. But do listen to and receive genuine compliments, encouragement, and words that build up faith. The more positive the people are around you, the easier it will be for you to remain positive about yourself and your goals.

Negative comments are like drops of indelible black ink put into a jar of crystal-clear water. They darken the soul and bring discouragement to the heart. Avoid negative influences and negative people as much as possible.

I recommend that you write some positive verses about God's help and provision on three-by-five-inch cards and keep them in your pocket or purse. Every time you hear negative comments, pull out one of those cards and read it. Don't let the negativity of others overwhelm you and capsize your dreams. Retaliate with the positive. If someone asks you what you are reading, share God's Word with him. You'll change your environment!

Look for a Personal Lesson in Every Defeat

Don't waste time wringing your hands or bemoaning your mistakes or losses. Look for a positive lesson to learn in times of failure or defeat. Don't look for excuses, justifications, or rationales. Grow from your mistakes.

Practice Self-Control

Choose to rule your emotions rather than let your emotions rule you. Don't work on the basis of your feelings—feelings come and go. Don't persist only when you feel like it. Take charge of your emotions. You do not need to waste valuable physical and emotional energy in anger, hatred, or bitterness. Neither do you need to waste valuable time in laziness and apathy.

Believe You Can Reach Your Goals

Persistence is directly linked to the strength of your beliefs. As I stated in the previous chapter, choose to believe that God is with you, God has a great reward ahead for you, and God will enable you to succeed in attaining it.

Rely on God to Enable You to Persevere

If you are feeling weak in your ability to persist, ask the Lord to renew your energy and your commitment to your goals. Ask God to infuse you with His power, strength, and ability.

God Will Not Give Up on You

God never gives up on you. His goal for your life is that you be conformed to the image of His Son (Rom. 8:29). God does not waver from His purposes and plans. Paul wrote to the Philippians, "He who has begun a good work in you will complete it until the day of Jesus Christ" (Phil. 1:6). God is never going to give up on the perfecting work He has started in you—and if for no other reason than that, you must never give up on God or the goals He has set before you.

Did God give up on you when you were a sinner? No.

Did God give up on you when you failed in your witness? No.

Did God give up on you when you strayed from Him and began to pursue your own desires? No.

Did God give up on you when you gave up in discouragement on the goals He gave you? No.

Will God ever give up on you? No!

He is always ready and eager to help you begin again, to start over, and to make another attempt. He is always ready to help you persist in the pursuit of His goals for your life. Turn to Him and receive the help He so generously offers.

CONCLUSION

~

Well-Ordered Steps

When do we decide that we will choose to succeed according to God's definition of *success*? It is a decision often made at moments of defeat.

It is when things seem to be going the wrong way, or when we seem to have hit rock bottom, that we tend to look around and say, "Nevertheless, I will trust God." So often when things are going our way, and we are experiencing rewards and positive results, we ignore the Lord. We take for granted His presence, provision, protection, and providence. If asked, we will say we trust God, but we rarely offer our spontaneous thanksgiving for His ongoing help and encouragement.

One of the most important marks of Christian maturity is an ongoing and continual recognition that the Lord is the One who makes possible all good things in our lives. Mature believers proclaim in all circumstances, "Every good and perfect gift comes from the Father" (see James 1:17).

Many of us make the decision to dig in our heels and obey God *in spite of what is happening around us*. It certainly is the stance we must take in times of failure as well as in times when we feel as if we are working hard and trusting God, yet things don't seem to be moving forward. We must affirm our faith in the Lord when times are tough. I also challenge you to

233

make a decision to trust in God and to obey Him when you are succeeding and things are going well for you! I challenge you to delight in praising God for His goodness to you when you feel successful, rewarded, appreciated, applauded, and accepted.

The Bible tells us,

> The steps of a good man are ordered by the LORD,
> And He delights in his way. (Ps. 37:23)

In good times and bad times, on mediocre days and exhilarating days, in periods of joy and periods of heavy toil, our stance before the Lord must be, "Heavenly Father, You're in charge. I have no success other than what You help me achieve. I trust You to order my steps."

I recently took a photography trip to a beautiful but fairly remote area of the United States. I had planned the trip for some time and was looking forward to my time alone with God and my camera in that beautiful location. When I arrived at my destination, however, and went to the car-rental booth, I discovered that I did not have my credit cards with me. I had just returned from an international trip and had failed to transfer my credit cards from my travel wallet to my regular wallet. I didn't have enough cash with me to secure a car, and I knew it would take at least a day—possibly two—for someone to gain authorized access to my home, find my travel wallet, and send a credit card to me. I was stuck. No car meant no photography trip into the mountains for a couple of days, which was a significant portion of my plans. I went to my hotel, but I didn't unpack.

Trying to figure out exactly what to do, I went down to the coffee shop, questioning God all the way, "Did I miss You on this? It seems to be a great waste of money to fly out here and not be able to do what I came here to do." Finally I concluded my conversation with the Lord, saying, "You're in charge."

A few moments later a man and a woman came over to my table and asked, "Are you Dr. Stanley?" I replied, "I am," and they introduced themselves. I invited them to join me, and as we conversed, I explained to them the problem I was facing. The man immediately responded, "That's no problem! You can take one of our cars for the week. We won't be using it, and we'd love for you to borrow it." And I did.

Not only did I have the use of a newer and nicer car than I would have rented, and at considerably less expense, but I gained a new friendship. I also learned once again that when we trust God with *all* things, He is faithful.

As I drove out into the mountains the next morning, I had intended to take one route, but found myself following another road with beautiful scenery so I stayed on it. It seemed at every bend in the road I came across another scene that I knew would make a good photograph. I had a great day meandering along the road, rarely seeing another vehicle. I stopped frequently to take photographs. "God, You're in charge" became not only a prayer, but a praise.

And then seemingly miles from nowhere without a soul in sight, I tried to start the car after one photography stop and discovered I was out of gas. Once again, I prayed, "God, You're in charge," and no sooner had I prayed than a man in a pickup pulled over next to my car and said, "Need some help?" I said, "I'm out of gas." He pointed down the road and said, "My truck is too dirty for you to get into it, but there's a gas station about a hundred yards from here, just around the next bend." Once again, God provided.

Was the trip a mistake? For about an hour after arriving at the airport I thought it was. It had all the outward earmarks of a defeat. Did God have something better in mind than I had planned? Absolutely. That time was one of the best I've ever experienced in photographing the Lord's handiwork.

Our walk on this earth is just that—a walk along a path. The prophet Micah said,

He has shown you, O man, what is good;
And what does the LORD require of you
But to do justly,
To love mercy,
And to walk humbly with your God? (Mic. 6:8)

Such a journey is a successful journey!
Moses asked,

What does the LORD your God require of you, but to fear the LORD your God, to walk in all His ways and to love Him, to serve the LORD your God with all your heart and with all your soul, and to keep the commandments of the LORD and His statutes which I command you today for your good? (Deut. 10:12–13)

Such a life is a successful life!
Trust God today to order each step you take toward the success He desires for you. Trust Him to order your steps and arrange all of the details of your journey as you walk in faith. If you are walking along God's chosen path for you, and you are trusting Him to order each step, you will be successful. Truly you will experience success—God's way!

ABOUT THE AUTHOR

Dr. Charles Stanley is pastor of the 14,000-member First Baptist Church in Atlanta, Georgia. He is well-known through his *In Touch* radio and television ministry to thousands internationally and is the author of many books, including *On Holy Ground, Our Unmet Needs, Enter His Gates, The Source of My Strength, The Reason for My Hope, How to Listen to God,* and *How to Handle Adversity.*

Dr. Stanley received his bachelor of arts degree from the University of Richmond, his bachelor of divinity degree from Southwestern Theological Seminary, and his master's and doctor's degrees from Luther Rice Seminary. He has twice been elected president of the Southern Baptist Convention.

OTHER BEST-SELLING BOOKS BY CHARLES STANLEY

Enter His Gates

Spiritual gates are much like the gates of a city. They are vital to your well-being as a Christian and, if not maintained, leave you open to attack by the enemy. *Enter His Gates* is a daily devotional that encourages you to build or strengthen a different spiritual gate each month.
0-7852-7546-0 • Hardcover • 400 pages • Devotional

In Touch with God

This unique gift book is filled with inspirational Scriptures as well as thoughts and prayers from Dr. Stanley. It will help you know God's heart on a variety of topics, including forgiveness, relationships, Spirit-filled living, Christian character, and God's plan for your life.
0-7852-7117-1 • Printed Hardcover • 208 pages • Gift/Devotional

On Holy Ground

This daily devotional contains a year's worth of spiritual adventures. Dr. Stanley uses the journeys of Paul, Ezra, Elijah, Abraham, and other heroes of the Bible and his own valuable insights to encourage you to step out in faith and allow God to lead you to new places.
0-7852-7662-9 • Hardcover • 400 pages • Devotional

The Power of the Cross

Using inspirational Scriptures as well as personal insights and heartfelt prayers, Charles Stanley encourages you to see the transforming power of the Resurrection for salvation, victory over temptation, healing of emotional pain, and restoration with the heavenly Father.

0-7852-7065-6 • Printed Hardcover • 208 pages • Gift/Devotional

The Reason for My Hope

Dr. Stanley shares his personal struggles to remain focused on Christ and keep hope alive in the middle of difficult circumstances. In his warm and insightful style, he reveals the promises and resources God provides His children, identifying nine key reasons for all believers to have unshakable hope.

0-8407-7765-5 • Hardcover • 256 pages • Christian Living